CW00470024

A Pianist's Glossary

Eric Smith has had a lifelong interest in the piano and piano music. He is the author of *Pianos in Practice* and *Pianos: Care and Restoration*. Eric Smith is married and lives in South Warnborough, Hampshire.

A
Pianist's
Glossary

ERIC SMITH

ROBERT HALE · LONDON

© *Eric Smith 1998*
First published in Great Britain 1998

ISBN 0 7090 6136 6

Robert Hale Limited
Clerkenwell House
Clerkenwell Green
London EC1R 0HT

The right of Eric Smith to be identified as
author of this work has been asserted by him
in accordance with the Copyright, Designs and
Patents Act 1988.

2 4 6 8 10 9 7 5 3 1

Photoset in North Wales by
Derek Doyle & Associates, Mold, Flintshire
Printed in Great Britain by
St Edmundsbury Press Limited, Bury St Edmunds
and bound by
WBC Book Manufacturers Limited, Bridgend

Contents

Acknowledgements

Grateful acknowledgement is made to Michael Cohen and my son, the late Graham Smith, and also to the co-operation of Dr Tom Messenger, Head of Music at the University of Surrey. I am also deeply indebted to the late William Gurney, formerly Professor of Pianoforte at the Guildhall School of Music and Drama, who inspired me at an early age with love of the piano. Naturally I retain full responsibility for whatever deficiencies there may be in this little guide.

Preface

This pianist's glossary is, first and foremost, a dictionary. It translates and defines the words and short phrases by which composers, mainly in Italian, French, German, or Spanish, indicate how their work is to be played – speed, volume, mood. Certain other words – mainly titles and musical forms – are included because their choice also impinges on interpretation.

The book has another aspect also, which is manifested in the copious references given for words and phrases. This is the consideration by comparison of how composers have used this language of instruction to performers. For example, it helps you to distinguish what is a favourite or characteristic expression of one composer, but not of another, or whether an expression is particularly common at a certain time or in a certain musical form, or how this language has developed historically. Equally, you may find that a particular directive is extremely rare or used by only one composer. In general, the scope of the glossary coincides with the trend towards 'expressiveness' in both directives and instrumental design from the later eighteenth century onwards.

Entries under the words 'innig' and 'sciolto' exemplify information of this specific sort. Beethoven, followed by Schumann, reserved 'innig' ('inwardly') for a few late pieces of especially introspective music, and it was seldom adopted by any other composer. The term 'sciolto' ('nimbly, with agility') is used in the fourteenth Variation of the great set which Brahms wrote on a theme by Handel (Op.24). It is almost unrecorded in the dictionaries and, to the best of my knowledge, was otherwise used only by Liszt (twice).

You are able to draw such conclusions here because the choice of word-entries is not random or derived from assumed frequency of use, but based on a complete index of the work of the listed composers, from the late eighteenth century to the present time (excluding those now living).

The historical boundaries do, of course, need defence. It has long been a custom among anthologies of literary and other work to exclude living writers. It may be felt, for example, that the work in question represents, however loosely, some sort of 'canon' whose nature in contemporary terms may come to seem invidious or even embarrassing in the future, or disproportionately weighted towards the contemporary where knowledge is so much greater. Whilst it may entail interrupting a development towards ever-greater explicitness in authorial directions which is manifestly still under way, I still do not therefore feel great misgivings in curtailing this book by excluding living composers.

But the other end – that is, before the late eighteenth century – does cause more problems, for how representational can be a coverage which for the most part excludes such as Haydn, Mozart, the Bachs, the Scarlattis, Rameau ... to name but a few?

There are three reasons for such exclusions. In the first place there is the transition, most obvious in Beethoven's work, between the clavichord, the harpsichord and the piano itself; to an uncertain degree, authorial directions would have been written for instruments only in some degree relevant to the piano as we know it. Secondly, the directions are not, in general, there; for it was the custom to give little more than plain indications of speed – which are covered (though without these particular examples) in the glossary anyway. Bach (JS) himself felt it necessary to explain how this indication of 'ornaments' – the other field which could be copiously illustrated but which has to be outside our scope – was geared to his (at that time somewhat remarkable) objective of obtaining a true 'cantabile' from instruments other than the piano as it was to become. Haydn in his later work did tend to become somewhat more 'expressive', but not in a consistent thoroughness with words other than those already covered in the glossary as it is. On the whole, the performer of music from these earlier periods is either on his own or plunged into a thicket of controversy, neither of which is really helpful to my purpose, even if the result may seem foreshortened.

Then, in the third place, we must be concerned as far as possible with authentic authorial directions, and the difficulty in establishing authenticity naturally increases as we go back in time. Either necessary autographs do not exist, or they have been bowdlerized by the imaginations of later editors. I conclude, therefore, that, so far as the *piano* goes, we are better served by a glossary of directions certainly written for that instrument, while yet covering the earlier period by a dictionary of simple form.

Conventions followed

1. Entries

Words are always indexed as they occur, not by reference to their grammatical roots such as nominatives and infinitives. This makes for some repetition, but also for easier reference – it would not be helpful to have to find 'dasselbe' under 'derselbe'. I think that such conveniences should outweigh purist linguistic considerations.

A further convention is that a bracket number after an Opus number refers to the number of the movement or part in which the usage occurs. When, quite rarely, Opus numbers are divided into works which may themselves have several parts, these major divisions have been numbered distinctively (e.g. 'Beeth. Son.Op.2 No.1(2), refers to the Slow Movement of Beethoven's first Sonata, which is one of three in his Opus 2.

When a literal translation or linguistic origin is tangentially related to normal musical usage, the translation is given in brackets, e.g. **Adagio** (at ease) slow.

Where the entry-expression is repeated (for example as part of a phrase) it is designated by —.

Words interrupted by spaces (e.g. accelerando … a tempo) repeat the layout in the score and indicate continuation of the first instruction until the second.

2. Frequency of Expressions and References

For the commonest instructions no reference may be given. It

11

would serve little purpose to accumulate references to 'allegro' or to purely grammatical words like prepositions. Similarly, notational directives, such as appoggiatura, are not included.

Entries for very common words and phrases list the composers (rather than specific works) where they are found. More specific references are given for the less common expressions.

Where such references number no more than two, they are all that have been found. If they exceed two, a selection has been made. Thus a single reference (unless marked 'e.g.') can be assumed to be the only one found. Directives particularly used by certain composers have the composers distinguished by asterisk (*).

Throughout, attention has been given to combinations of words in sometimes characteristic phrases. The formulation 'A but not B' (e.g. 'allegro ma non troppo', 'forte ma dolce') is a much used part of this language of composers. The same guides as to frequency apply also to these and other multiple expressions.

While it has not been possible to pursue autographs of so large a volume of music, every other effort has been made to exclude editorial directions.

3. Abbreviations and titles

Titles of pieces and collections are generally indicated in italic type (e.g. *Wiegenlied*) unless clearly generic (e.g. Sonata). There are cases where both title and genus are involved (e.g. Chopin Nocturnes), but here, as with all marginal generic terms, the title is not italicized.

Abbreviations for frequently occurring titles, composers and genres are listed at the back of the book (page 93).

——— A ———

a (It.) à (Fr.) at, to, with

abbandonandosi (It.) abandoned, free: Liszt *Liebestraum* **quasi-lento** — slowly, and freely

abbandono (It.) abandoned: Chopin Noct.Op.62(1); Liszt *3 Concert Studies* (1); Gran. *Esc.Rom* (1) **con** — with abandonment, freely, passionately

abbellimenti (It.) ornaments

Abendlied (Ger.) evening song: Schum. *Son. Für die Jugend* Op.118(2)

abnehmend (Ger.) ('taking away') reducing volume: Schum. *Son. Für die Jugend* Op.118(2)

a capriccio (It.) capriciously, whimsically: Liszt *Soir.*(6). *See* **capriccio**

accarezzevole (It.) caressingly: Scriabin Son.Op.53(1)

acc ... al tempo (It.) speed up, then return to time: Bartók *Mikro.*(46), (2 cycles)

accel(erando) (It.) accelerating: e.g. Elgar *Allegro* Op.46

accentato (It.) accented, stressed: Liszt* *Consolation* (2) **appassionato e molto** —; *Liebesträume* (1) **il canto** — **assai**; *EET*(10) — **ed apassianato assai**; *3 Concert Studies* (1) **la melodia** — **assai**; — **il canto**; Son.(3) B Min., *Tannhäuser Overt.*, *Lugubre Gondola* (3)

accentuata (It.) stressed, accentuated: e.g. Liszt *HPR*(7) **La melodia sempre** —

accentuato (It.) stress, emphasis; Liszt *A de P*23 — **il canto**; Liszt *A de P*3 **molto** —

accompagnement (Fr.) accompaniment: Poulenc Noct. (1) **l'** — **très estompé et regulier,** the accompaniment blurred and regular

13

accompagnamento (It.) accompaniment: Liszt* e.g. *HPR*(3) — **semper sotto voce e legato**, the accompaniment always subdued and even; *HPR*(2) — **pesante**, the accompaniment heavy; Brahms *Schum.Var.Op.9*(10)

accord/Akkord (Fr., Ger.) chord: Medtner Op.1(5) **Diesen — nicht schlagen**, do not strike this chord

Accordwechsel (Ger.) change of chord: Liszt *12 Grandes Études* (1)

acht (Ger.) eight

acuratezza (It.) accurately: Schum. *Abegg Var.*(3) **con** — with care, diligence

acuto (It.) sharp, intense: Deb. Études (7)

adagietto (It.) slightly faster (and lighter) than **adagio**: Strav. Son.(1924)(2)

adagio (It.) 'at ease', slow (but less slow than **largo**). Next above **adagietto, andante**; next below **larghetto.**

ad lib(itum) (L.) freely: Bartók, Beeth., Brahms, Clementi, Deb., Liszt, Rach., Satie, Schum., Scriabin; Brahms Cadenza for Mozart *D min.Conc.* — **recitativisch**; — **quasi sensa tempo**, without adhering to a set tempo; Franck *Eclogue* Op.3 — **espressivo** — Gran. *Goy.*(6)

a due (It.) in two melodic parts, two voices to be brought out: Schum. *Et. Symph.* Op.13 **quasi** — as if in two distinct parts

aérien (Fr.) aerial, very light: Deb. Prél.1(2)

affanato (It.) breathlessly, winded: Scriabin Son.Op.53(1) **sotto voce misterioso** — subdued and breathlessly mysterious

affetto (It.) feeling: Beeth., Chopin, Kuhlau, Liszt, Schum., Scriabin, **con** — with feeling

affetuoso (It.) affectionately, tenderly: Scriabin Prél.Op.11(19); Liszt *3 Concert Studies* (3)

affretando (It.) hurrying, impatiently: e.g. Liszt *Liebesträume* (3); Barber Son.(3); Liszt *3 Concert Studies* (1); Albéniz *Iberia* **poco** —, slightly hurrying

affretare (It.) hurry: **non** —, Bach/Busoni *Chaconne*

agevole (It.) easily, smoothly: Scriabin *Valse* Op.38

agitatissimo (It.) extremely agitated, manic: Prok. Op.22(19) **presto** — **e molto accentuato**, very fast, agitated and stressed

agitato (It.) restlessly, with agitation: Beeth; Chopin* Franck, Hindemith, Liszt, Martinů, Medtner, Schum.; Brahms

Var.Op.21(1) **espressivo** —; Mn *SWW* (46) **un poco — ma Andante;** — Liszt *12 Grandes Études* (8) — **ed appassionata assai**

agitazione (It.) agitation, disturbance: Brahms Son.Op.2(3) **con molto —, sempre molto sostenuto;** Liszt *Tannhäuser Overt.*, trs. Schub. 'Sei mir gegrüsst', *12 Grandes Études* (11) **grandioso senza —,** *EETF*(6) **con —**

agité (Fr.) agitated, excited: Poulenc Imp.1, **très —**

agitirt (Ger.) disturbed, **agitato:** Schum. *Alb.Y.*(25)

Agosto (It.) August

agrandissement asymétrique (Fr.) broadening asymetrically, with an unpatterned, improvisatory character: Messiaen *VR*3,6

Ahnung (Ger.) foreboding, presentiment: Schum. *Albumb* 'Liedes —', forebodings of pain/suffering

aigu (Fr.) sharp, intense, acute: Scriabin *Poèmes*

ailé (Fr.) winged, flying: Scriabin *Morceau* Op.51(3), Son.Op.62, Op.70

airoso (It.) breezy: Gran. *Goy*(2), *Danses* (60)

aise (Fr.) ease: Deb. Prél.2(8), **a l' —,** comfortably, freely; Poulenc *Improvisations* (15)

aisément (Fr.) easily, freely: Albéniz *Iberia* ('El Puerto')

a(l) (It.) to

à l'Allemande (Fr.) in the German manner: Beeth., Bag.Op.119(3). German dance in triple time and moderate speed. (Historically a slower dance in duple time starting with a 'loose' note.)

Alborada del Gracioso (Sp.) dawn music/aubade for the (court) fool

Albumblätter (Ger.) pages from an album: Schum: Op.124, title, *cf* **feuillet**

alegremente (Sp.) happily: Albéniz Op.47(8)

alenti (Fr.) slowed down: Ravel *Menuet Antique* **à peine —,** slightly slowed

alla (It.) with, by, to, at, in: Beeth.: 10 Var.(1799) — **Austrica,** in the Austrian manner; Scriabin *Études* op.8(9) — **ballata,** as a dance; Mouss. *Pict.*(10) — **Breve,** in breves, a slow duple time in which the minim rather than the crotchet is the rhythmic unit. Historically the unit was a 'breve' (eight crotchets) rather than a semibreve, which was half a breve or four crotchets. It is notated with the signs ₵ or $\frac{2}{2}$. The effect is usually solemn, spacious, grand; — **Burla**, in joke, in fun, *see* **burla**; Beeth. Var.Op.35, — **Fuga**, in the manner of a fugue; Beeth. Son.Op.101(2) — **Marcia**, in march time; Scriabin Son.Op.68; — **Polacca**, in the manner of a Polonaise; Beeth. Son.Op.79(1) — **Tedesca**, in the German style, sometimes that of an *allemande*: later more often that of a Waltz or Ländler (Tedesca = Teutonic)

allant (Fr.) going, moving: Deb. Prél.2(2) **un peu plus** — going a little faster; Poulenc Noct. **trés** — (2), **assez** — (6)

allargamente (It.) broadening, becoming slower and fuller: Satie *Valse Ballet* Op.62

allarg(ando) (It.) broadening, becoming slower and fuller: Bartók, Busoni, Chopin, Clementi, Deb., Elgar, Fauré, Hindemith, Ireland, Medtner, Mouss. Prok., Scriabin, Sibelius, Smetana, Scho.; Bartók *Mikro.* **pochissima** —; Barber *Excursion* — **sine alla fine**, broadening until the end, Son.(4) — **il meno possible**, broadening as little as possible

allegramente (It.) becoming fast, lively, fairly fast: Beeth; Bag.Op.119 (10); Liszt *Valse Oubliée* (2)

allegretto (It.) fairly fast/lively (diminutive of **allegro**); next above **allegro**, next below **moderato**: Beeth. Son.Op.31 (3) — **vivace**, quite fast, with spirit (also Clementi Son.Op.39(3)); Dussek Op.19(2) — **non troppo**; Liszt *Apparitions* — **senza lentezza**, without slowness, **quasi** —; Mn *SWW* Op.67(6) — **non troppo**; Tch. Op.19(3) — **simplice**; Schub. Son.Op.164 — **quasi andantino**

allegrezza (It.) cheerfulness, sprightliness: Mouss. *Pict.*; Scriabin Son.Op.53(1), Son.Op.53(1) **con** —, cheerfully

allegrissimo (It.) extremely fast. Next above **presto**, next below **allegro**

allegro (It.) fast, bright, merry: Clementi Son.Op.50(3) — **ma con expressione**; Dussek Op.19(3) — **quasi presto**; Mn Op.84 — **assai vivace**; — **assai/assai** —, very fast

allemande (Fr.) moderately slow and serious German dance in duple time, developed in instrumental suites throughout Europe

allmählich (Ger.) gradually, by degrees

allontanosi/allontandosi (Ger.) fading into the distance: Gottschalk *Berceuse*

allora (It.) then

alouette (Fr.) lark

al rovescio (It.) in reverse (e.g. as a palindrome, the tune played backward from the end) Haydn Son.A maj.(1773)

al tempo (It.) in the original time

alternativo (It.) an option in the sequence of **minuet** and **trio**

altieramente (It.) proudly: Liszt *HR*4

alzando (It.) (mutes, dampers) raised, use sustaining pedal: Prok. Son.3(1)

amabilita (It.) pleasantness, amiability: Beeth. Son.Op.110(1) *see* con —

âme (Fr.) mind, soul: Satie *Danses Gothiques*

Ammenmärchen (Ger.) nurse's tale: Tch. Op.39(18)

amore (It.) love: Busoni *Fanta. on Carmen* con —, with love

amorosamente (It.) affectionately: Liszt*; Gran. *Esc.Poet.*(1)

amoroso (It.) lovingly, affectionately, amorously: Liszt*, Scriabin, Tch.; *Goy*.2, 5 con sentimento —

amour (Fr.) love: mystérieux, avec —; Messiaen *VR*1

ampiezza (It.) breadth: de Falla *Noches en los jardines de España*(3) con —, with breadth, amply

ancora (It.) still, again

andando (It.) moving, with gentle motion: Busoni *Fanta. Contrappuntistica*

andante (It.) ('going') moving gently, at walking pace. Next above **andantino**, next below **adagietto**: Fauré *Imp.*Op.91 — molto moderato quasi adagio; Mn Op.35(5) — lento; Liszt, *A de P*2(7) — maestoso

andantino (It.) less/more slowly than **andante**. Next above **moderato**, next below **andante**; Gran. *Goy*.(2) — allegretto

an der Wiege (Ger.) by the cradle, like a lullaby

Anfang (Ger.) beginning

angoisse (Fr.) anguish; **angoissé** anguished, distressed: Deb. Prél.1(7)

angoscioso (It.) anguished: Liszt trs. Schub. 'Meeresstille'

anima (It.) life, spirit, animation: Albéniz, Chopin, Liszt, Mn, Scriabin con —, lively, with spirit

animando (It.) becoming more lively: Britten, Gran., Medtner; Liszt *A de P,* 1(3) sempre — sino al fine, more and more lively until the end

animant (Fr.) lively, en —, becoming more lively

animato (It.) with animation: Gran. *Goy*.(4) — e dramatico animé (Fr.) lively

animez (Fr.) become lively: Deb. *Su.Berg.*(6); Poulenc *Hymne*

anmutig (Ger.) graceful; Brahms Op.76(3)(8)

années (Fr.) years: Liszt, — de Pèlerinage', title, years of pilgrimage

Anschlag (Ger.) striking blow: Scho. Op.103(7)

anschlagen (Ger.) to strike, sound, play a note: Scho. Op.25 nochmals — play again

ansioso (It.) anxious: Busoni *Fanta. Contrappuntistica*

Antwort (Ger.) answer

apaisant (Fr.) pacifying, becoming calm: Deb. *Images* (2) en s' —, growing calm

apaisé (Fr.) made peaceful. Deb. Prél.1(2)

à peine (Fr.) hardly: Satie *Gymnopédie* (2) ralentir —, slow down very slightly

apertamente (It.) openly: Busoni *Son'a ad usum infantis* (4)

a piacere (It.) at pleasure, pleasingly, 'ad libitum', 'if you wish': Chopin*, Clementi, Fauré, Gran., Haydn, Liszt*, Medtner, Scriabin, Sibelius; Bach/Busoni *Chaconne* un poco — ma sempre energico il ritmo, a little freely but keeping the strong rhythm; Chopin Prél.Op.45 cadenza —; Gran. *Goy.*(1) quasi a tempo molto —, in time but with great freedom

à plat (Fr.) flat out: Scriabin *Danses de Travers* (1)

appassionata/o (It.) impassioned, with feeling: Liszt*, Gran.

appassionatamente (It.) passionately: Gran. *Esc.Rom.*(2)

appel (Fr.) appeal: Scriabin Son.Op.62 — mystérieux

appuyé (Fr.) (supported) sustained: Deb. *Images* (2)

arabesk/arabeque (Fr.) fantastic, twirling, originally with an oriental flavour: name for a short fanciful piece, e.g. by Schum., Grieg

à quattro (It.) in four parts: Beeth. Var.Op.35

arbre (Fr.) tree: title, 'Sur Un —

arc-en-ciel (Fr.) rainbow: Prok. Op.65 (8); Messiaen *VR*(16)

ardamente (It.) passionately: Liszt *Apparitions*

ardentamente (It.) ardently, passionately: Liszt tr. Schub. 'Die Junge Nonne'

ardeur (Fr.) passion: Scriabin Son.Op.70 avec une — profonde et voilée, with a deep and hidden passion

ardito (It.) bravely, with daring: Scriabin Prél.Op.33(4); Liszt trs. *Tannhäuser Overt., Ballade* (2)

aria (It.) air, tune, song

arietta (It.) diminutive of aria, small air, song: Beeth. Son.Op.111(2); Clementi Son.Op.24(3); cf. **arioso**

arioso (It.) song-like, as a song: Beeth. Son.Op110(3) — **dolente**, sad song; Hindemith *Ludus Tonalis*

arm(es) (Ger.) poor, pitiable: Schum; *Alb.Y.*(6); Mouss. *Pict*(6)

armonioso (It.) harmoniously: Albéniz, Franck, Gottschalk, Liszt*

arpa (It.) harp (usually in the phrase '**quasi —**', 'like a harp'): Busoni *Fanta.Contrappuntistica*; Prok. Op.22(7); Grieg Op.50: Liszt* trs. *Tannnhäuser Overt*. **quasi — una corda**, like a harp, with soft pedal

arpèges (Fr.) arpeggios

arpeggiando (It.) Liszt* *see* **arpeggiato**

arpeggiato (It.) spread as an arpeggio (of chords): Sho. PF Op.87(5); Liszt*

arpeggio (It.) the notes of a chord fanned in an upward or (less often) downward pattern, like those on a harp (**arpa**)

arraché (Fr.) snatched: Messiaen *Fd d J*, VR18

arrêt (Fr.) stop(ping): **sans —**, without stopping

articolando (It.) articulating, separated: Medtner Op.11(2)

Artico/ulato (It.) articulated: Liszt*; Barber *Tango* Op.28; Bach/Busoni *Chaconne* — **assai**

articula (Fr.) articulated: Poulenc *Suite* **uniformément — et fort**, regularly and strongly articulated

aspiramente (It.) breathingly, as a sigh

assai (It.) very, a lot

assez (Fr.) enough, fairly: **— vif**, rather lively, **— animé**, fairly lively

à travers (Fr.) through, across

a tre (It.) in three parts or voices (to be brought out): Beeth. Var.Op.35

attaca (It.) attack: **— subito**, attack directly, go straight on to the next movement

attendre (Fr.) to wait

attenué (Fr.) attenuated, reduced: Deb. Prél.1(2); Albéniz *Iberia*

attrape qui peut (Fr.) 'catch-as-catch-can', 'he' (children's game): Prok. Op.65(9)

aubade (Fr.) dawn serenade

aucun(e) (Fr.) any

au début (Fr.) in the beginning, at first

au-dessous (Fr.) under, below: Deb. Prél.1(7) **commencer un peu — de mouvement,** start a little below the desired speed

aufgeregt (Ger.) excited, agitated: Brahms Op.76(5) **sehr —, doch nicht zu schnell,** very agitated but not too fast

auflebend (Ger.) reviving: Beeth. Son.Op.110(3)

au flot (Fr.) like a wave: Satie *Poésie*

Aufruf zum Kampf (Ger.) call to battle; Liszt *Fanta. on 'Rienzi'*

Aufschwung (Ger.) soaring, flight: Schum. *Fant.* Op.12

Auftakt (Ger.) 'up' beat

augmentez (Fr.) increase speed and/or volume

aurore (Fr.) dawn

Ausdruck (Ger.) expression: Beeth. Son.Op81a(2) **in gehender Bewegung, doch mit —,** at a fair speed but with expression; Beeth. Son.Op.90(1); Scho. Op.23 **etwas ruhiger im —,** somewhat quieter in expression: Scho.Op.19(6) **mit sehr zartem —,** with a very tender expression

ausdrucksvoll (Ger.) full of expression: Brahms Op.76(3); Schum. Son.Op.118(3)(7)

ausgeschlüpften Kücken (Ger.) hatched-out chicks: Mouss. *Pict.*(5)

äusserst (Ger.) exceptionally, extremely: Brahms Son.Op.5 (2) **— leise und zart,** very gentle and tender; Schum. *Nov.* Op.21(2) **— rasch und mit bravour,** extremely fast and with bravura

ausser tempo (Ger.) out of time, *see* **rubato** Schum. Hum.Op.20

aussi (Fr.) as: **— ...quo,** *as ... as;* Deb. *Éstampes* (1) **— pp que possible,** as quiet as possible

Ausstellung (Ger.) exhibition

au temps (Fr.) in time

avec (Fr.) with

avec étonnement (Fr.) with astonishment: Satie *Gnossienne* (2)

avec force (Fr.) with force, strongly: Satie *Gnossienne* (4) **— et expression**

avec la petite pédale (Fr.) with very little (sustaining) pedal: Albéniz *Iberia*

——B——

Bächlein (Ger.) streamlet, brook

Bagatelle (Ger.) a trifle, (which may be profound); Beeth., title, — Op.33, 119, 126

baigné (Fr.) swimming with, dripping with: Poulenc *Novelette* (3) — **des pédales**, swamped with pedal

bailada (Sp.) dance, dancing

baiser (Fr.) kiss; Messiaen *VR15*

bald (Ger.) soon

ballabile (It.) like a dance or ball: Deb. *Études* (3) — **e grazioso**, like a dance and graceful

ballademässig (Ger.) in ballad time, broad and flexible: Schum. *Davidsbündler* (10)

ballmässig (Ger.) dancelike: Schum. *Nov.*Op.21 (4)

barcarolle (Fre.) a piece in triple time (6/8, 12/8 e.g.) with a gentle swing (originally a boat song): Chopin Op.60; Fauré Op.26 etc; Tch. Op.37a(6)

barque (Fr.) ship

bassa (It.) bassa. 8° — an octave below that written

basses (Fr.) bass notes: Deb. *Études* (6) **les** — **légèrement expressives**, the lower notes lighly expressive

basso (It.) the bass part

batteries (Fr.) blows, beats: Poulenc Noct.(8) **les** — **très discrètes**, the bass subdued

battute (It.) bar, beat

Bauer (Ger.) peasant: Tch. Op.39; Dvořák Op.85(5), title, **'Bauernballade'**

Bauernlied (Ger.) peasants' song

beaucoup (Fr.) a lot, much, a great deal

bedeutet (Ger.) means: Schollum 7 *fantasies*

beginnen (end) (Ger.) begin: Scho. Op. 29 **langsam** — starting slowly

Begleitung (Ger.) accompaniment

Begräbnis (Ger.) burial, interment: Tch. Op.39(24)

beiden (Ger.) both

belebt (Ger.) lively: Schum. *Albumb.* Op.133(39)

bellicoso (It.) aggressively, pugnaciously: Scriabin Prél.Op.33(4)

21

belliqueux (Fr.) belligerent, aggressive: Scriabin Prél.Op.59(2), Op.74(5)

ben (It.) well; — **marcato**, well marked: Liszt *A de P*,7 — **marcato il canto**, the tune well stressed: — **cantato**, very songlike

berceuse (Fr.) rocking song, lullaby

bergamasque (Fr.) originally masked Italian dance in duple time: Deb. 'Suite —', - used evocatively with allusion to Verlaine's poem 'Clair de Lune', which refers to masked dances, bergamasques and lutes

Bergen (Ger.) mountains, hills

Berger (Ger.) shepherd

beschleunigt (Ger.) accelerating, precipitating: Scho. Op.11(3)

Beschluss (Ger.) conclusion, end

besinnlich (Ger.) reflective, contemplative: Schollum *7 Fantasies* (1)

bestimmt (Ger.) decisive, spoken decisively: Schum. *Alb*.Y.(23) **kurz und** —, staccato and decisively

Betonung (Ger.) tone, sound: Liszt Fanta.Op.2 **mit starker** —, with fuller tone

betrachten (Ger.) consider, regard

beweglich (Ger.) lively, with movement: Mn Op.7(4)

bewegt (Ger.) moved: **leise** —, gently moving; Berg Son.Op.1 **mässig** —, in moderate time; Hindemith Son.1(1) **ruhig** —; Brahms Op.76(1) **unruhig** —, with disturbed movement

Bewegung (Ger.) motion, movement: Beeth. Son.Op.81a **in gehender** —, **doch mit Ausdruck**, at a fair speed but with expression; Beeth. Bag.Op.119(6) **dieselbe** —, at the same speed; Mn Op.7(2) **mit heftiger** —, with vigorous motion

bienheureux (Fr.) happy, blest

Bild(er) (Ger.) picture

biond(in)a (It.) fair, blonde

bis (Ger.) until

bittendes (Ger.) imploring: Schum. *Ksz*.(4)

bizarre (Fr.) strange, odd; Scriabin *Poème* Op.63(1)

blanc (Fr.) white: Satie *Le Fils des Étoiles* **en** — **et immobile**, transparent and still

Blätter (Ger.) leaves, pages

Bömisch (Ger.) Bohemian

Botschaft (Ger.) message: Schum *Albumb*.(18)

bourrée (Fr.) French dance in quadruple time, usually beginning off the beat

bout (Fr.) end: Poulenc *Improvisations* (14) **d'un — à l'autre**, from beginning to end

bras (Fr.) arm(s): Messiaen *VR15*

Brautlied (Ger.) wedding song: Grieg Op.17(6)

Brautzeug (Ger.) bridal procession

bravour (Ger.) bravura, brilliance: Schum. *Nov.*Op.21(2) **äusserst rasch und mit —**, extremely fast and with bravura

bravura (It.) brilliance, bravura, display of skill: Bach/Busoni, Chopin, Gran., Liszt*, Schum.

breit(er) (Ger.) (more) broadly: Scho. Op.11(3), Op.33(6) Berg Son.1

Bremse (Ger.) gadfly

brevis (It.) short

brillant (Fr.) brilliant: Chopin, Ravel, Saint-Saëns, Satie, Scriabin; Poulenc *Improvisations* (12) **très — et très animé**

brillante (It.) brilliant: Albéniz, Barber, Beeth. Busoni, Chopin*, Elgar, Franck, Gottschalk, Gran., Liszt*, Scriabin, Schum.*, Tch.

brillantissimo (It.) very brilliant: Britten *Holiday Diary* (3)

brio (It.) vigour, brightness: Beeth., Chopin, Haydn, Liszt, Mouss., Prok. **con —**, with vigour, energy

brioso (It.) energetically, vigorously: Grieg, Liszt*, Medtner, Prok., Scriabin

brouillard (Fr.) fog, mist

brouillé (Fr.) blurred, confused: Messiaen *VR6* **très — de pédale**, very blurred by the pedal; *VR20* **— de pédale**

bruant juane (Fr.) yellow-hammer: Messiaen *FdJ*

bruit (Fr.) noise: Satie *Danses de Travers* (3)

brume (Fr.) mist, fog: Deb. Prél.1(10) **dans une — doucement sonore**, in a sweet-sounding mist

bruscamente (It.) abruptly: Scriabin Prél.Op.49(2) **— irato**, abruptly angry

brusque (Fr.) brusque, abrupt: Albéniz, Poulenc; Deb. Prél. **Avec des — oppositions d'extrême**, with extreme abrupt clashes

brusquement (Fr.) brusquely, abruptly: Albéniz *Iberia* 'El Puerto'

brusquerie (Fr.) abruptness, roughness: Albénix *Iberia* **sans —**

bruyant (Fr.) noisy: Albéniz *Iberia* **toujours joyeux et —**, always jolly and noisy

bueé (Fr.) mist, steam, vapour: Deb. *Images* 2(1) **comme une —**

irisée, like a luminous mist

Bulgarian Rhythm a rhythm in which the units of the bar are of varying lengths (e.g. 4+2+3 quavers): Bartók

bunte (Ger.) varied: Schum., title, ' — **Blätter**', varied pages

burla (It.) joke, fun: Grieg Op.19(2) **alla** —, in fun; Schum. Son.Op.11(3) **alla — ma pomposo**, as a joke, but weightily

burlando (It.) jokingly: Medtner Op.1(6)

burlesco (It.) burlesque, jesting: Kuhlau Son.9

Bursch (Ger.) boy, lad

byldo (Polish) Polish farm-cart: Mouss. *Pict.*

—— **C** ——

cachée (Fr.) hidden: Scriabin Op.53(1) **avec une douceur** —, with a hidden sweetness

cadencioso (It.) falling away: Gran. *Danses*(9)

cadenza (It.) a show-passage without accompaniment, often before a Coda, **quasi** —, a similar, less formal display passage: Chopin, Clementi, Deb.*, Liszt*, Scriabin, Schum.*; Liszt Pol.(1) **quasi — improvisata**

cahier (Fr.) notebook, exercise book: Deb., title, '**D'un — d'Esquisses**', from a book of sketches

caille (Fr.) quail

calando (Fr.) failing, fading away: Bartók, Bn*, Brahms, Busoni, Chopin*, Clementi*, Dussek, Field, Gran., Liszt*, Medtner, Prok., Rach., Schub., R. Strauss; Liszt *Soir.*(1), (4) **poco — a piacere, — e smorzando**, falling away at will and extinguishing

calmant (Fr.) calming: Deb. *Éstampes* (3) **en se** —, calming down

calmante (It.) becoming calm: Britten *Holiday Diary* (2)

calmato (It.) calmed, calmly: Britten, Chopin, Deb., Gran., Liszt*, Busoni *Carmen Fantasy*, **— e sumando**, growing calm and still; Liszt trs. Schub. 'Die Junge Nonne' **— religiosamente**

calme (Fr.) calm: Messiaen, Poulenc, Ravel, Satie; Albéniz *Iberia* **plus — e sempre cantando**; Poulenc *Pastorale* **— et mystérieux**

calmo (It.) calm, even: Bartók, *Mikro.*35, 79; Busoni *Fanta. Contrappuntistica*

calore (It.) warmth: Scriabin *Poème* Op.32(2); Busoni *Fanta. Contrappuntistica* con —, warmly

caloroso (It.) warmly: Prok. Son.Op.83(2)

campagnard (Fr.) rural, pastoral

campana (Sp.) bells

campanella (It.) little bell: Liszt trs. Schub. 'Das Sterben Glöcklein'; *HR*11 **piano quasi** —, quiet as a little bell

cancion (Sp.) song: Gran. *Danses* (4); Albéniz Op.47(4)

candidement (Fr.) frankly, clearly. Satie *Danses de Travers*

canin (Fr.) canine: Satie *Prél.Canin*

canon (L.) a movement in which one voice strictly imitates another, from which it is separated by a fixed distance in time and pitch

canonisch (Ger.) in canon form

cantabile (It.) singing, songlike: Bartók, Beeth.*, Britten, Busoni, Chopin*, Clementi, Elgar, Fauré, Franck, Field, Grieg, Haydn, Ireland, Kuhlau, Liszt, Lut., Martinů, Medtner, Mn., Mouss., Mozart, Prok., Rach.*, Scho., Schub., Schum., Scriabin*, Strav., Tch.; Beeth. Son.Op.101(1) **molto** — **dolce ed espressivo**; Op.111(1) **semplice e** —, Rondo Op,51(2) — **e grazioso**; Clementi Son.Op.25(1) **maestoso e** — Field Son.Op.1(1) — **sempre legato**; Franck *Prel. Aria, Fugue,* **molto** — **il basso**; Grieg Op.43(6) — **e molto tenuta la melodia**; Op.19(3) **tranquillo e** —; Liszt *HPR*(2) — **assai e con passione,** *Robert le Diable* — **appassionato**; Mn *SWW*(42) **sempre** — **la melodia**

cantando (It.) singing, songlike: Albéniz, Barber, Brahms, Fauré, Franck, Gran., Grieg, Janáček, Liszt*, Medtner; Albéniz Op.47(4) — **largamente ma dolce**; Gran. *Goy.*(2) — **molto expressivamente**; Liszt *Sunt Lacrimae Rerum* — **e legatissimo**; *Consolation* (2), — **espressivo**; *Polonnaise* (1) **ben** — **ma semplice**

cantato (It.) sung: Albéniz Op.47(4)

canto (It.) song, tune, part: Chopin, Liszt, Mouss., Schum., Scriabin; Liszt *Liebesträume* (1, 2) **il** — **accentato assai**; Mouss. *Pict.* **il** — **cantabile, ben marcato**; Schum. *Ét. Symph.*(2) **marcato il** —, stress the tune

capo (It.) beginning, *see* **da** —

25

cappricciosa/omente (It.) capricious, whimsical: Liszt

capriccio(so) (It.) whim, caprice, musical piece of a whimsical character: Beeth., Brahms, Chopin, Fauré, Franck, Grieg, Liszt, Medtner, Men., Mouss., Mozart, Tch.; Medtner Op.11(1) **poco — ed irresoluto**, wayward and wavering; Schum. Son.Op.14(3), **molto a —**, very fanciful

capricieusement (Fr.) capriciously, whimsically: Scriabin Op.52(2)

caprisieux/se (Fr.) capricious, whimsical: Deb. *Images* (2) — **et souple**, capricious and supple; Scriabin *Poème*, Op.6 **avec une grâce capricieuse**

capricho (Sp.) whim: ˆAlbéniz Op.47(8)

caprizioso (Sp.) capricious, whimsical: Gran. *Goy.*(1)

caressant (Fr.) caressing: Deb. Prél.2(4); Albéniz *Iberia* **souple et —**; Scriabin Son.Op.68, **avec une douceur de plus en plus — et empoisonée,** with a sweetness more and more cloying and poisoned

carezzando (It.) caressing: Scriabin*, Medtner Op.11(1)

carnet (Fr.) notebook: Satie, title, '**— d'Esquisses**', book of drafts

carratteristicamente (It.) characteristically, idiosyncratically

Cataluna (Sp.) Catalonia

cédant (Fr.) reducing speed

céder (Fr.) give way, reduce speed

cédez (Fr.) reduce speed: Deb. *Études 5* **— ... mouvement,** yield, then back to time (twice); Ravel *Gaspard* (1) **— légèrement,** lightly slow down

céleste (Fr.) muted, a strip of felt which can be interposed between hammers and strings in many older pianos; there is no satisfactory modern substitute and the 'soft pedal' has to suffice: Gottschalk *Dying Poet* **gardez la pédale —,** keep the céleste pedal on

cembalo (It.) harpsichord: Beeth. Son.Op.101(3) **tutto il — ma piano,** with the whole instrument, all the strings, but quietly

cependant (Fr.) nonetheless, still

ceremonioso (It.) ceremoniously. Busoni *Son'a ad usum infantis*

certa (It.) certain: Beeth. Bag.Op.33(6)

chaconne (Fr.) **passacaglia** (It.) originally a slow, triple-time Spanish dance, but by the later seventeenth century denoting a composition developed over a recurring sequence of bass notes or ground bass

chaleur (Fr.) warmth: Scriabin Son.Op.62 **avec un — contenue,** with restrained warmth

chalumeaux (Fr.) pipes

champ (Fr.) field

chanson (Fr.) song

chant (Fr.) song, tune, musical part

chantant (Fr.) singing, songlike, *see* **cantabile:** Messiaen *VR*15 — très lié, singing, very smooth

chaque (Fr.) each

chardonneret (Fr.) goldfinch

charme (Fr.) charm, grace: Poulenc *Suite* (1920); Messiaen *VR*19

charmes (Fr.) charms, spells: Scriabin Son.Op.62

chasse (Fr.) hunt: Messiaen *VR*10

chasse-neige (Fr.) snow-plough

che (It.) than: Ireland Son. **meno mosso — el primo,** less movement than the first time

chiammando (It.) clear, distinct: Busoni *Son'a ad usum infantis*

chiaro (It.) clear: Britten Noct.; Busoni Son.

Choral (Ger.) German hymn: Mn. Op.35(2)

chuette hulotte (Fr.) tawny owl: Messiaen *FdJ*

clair (Fr.) clear

clair de lune (Fr.) moonlight: Deb. *Su.Berg.* (3), title

clarté (Fr.) clarity: Scriabin Son.Op.62

cloches (Fr.) bells: Messiaen *VR*2 **comme des —,** like bells

cloîtrement (Fr.) as in a cloister, religiously: Satie *Poésie*

coda (It.) tail, conclusion, finale, coda

col (It.) with: **— ped,** with sustaining pedal

colla parte (It.) solo part, tune: Liszt *Liebesträume* (1) **l'accompagnamento sempre pp e —,** accompaniment and solo part very quiet

collera (It.) anger. Scriabin Prél.Op.33(3) **con —,** angrily

colombe (Fr.) dove

coloquio en la Reja (Sp.) conversation at the grating/grille: Gran. *Goy.*(2)

col pugno (It.) with the fist: Prok. Son.Op.82(1)

come (It.) as, like: Rach. Son.Op.28(3) **— primo,** as the first time

comodetto (It.) easily, in a relaxed way: Beeth. 13 Var.(1792)

comme (Fr.) as, like

commencer (Fr.) begin

com(m)odo (It.) comfortable, relaxed, without strain: Albéniz.

Bartók, Beeth., Britten, Chopin, Medtner, Mouss., Poulenc, Prok., Rach., Schum., Tch., Strav.

commovente (It.) touching, moving, stirring: Busoni *Fanta. Contrappuntistica*

compiacevole (It.) pleasing, with contentment: Beeth. Bag.Op.126(1) **cantabile e —**

con (It.) with

concentré (Fr.) concentratd, intense: Scriabin Son.Op.62 **mysterieux, —**

confus (Fr.) confused

con mortuis in lingua mortua (L.) with the dead, in the language of the dead: Mouss. *Pict.*(8)

conseillez-vous soigneusement (Fr.) be scrupulous, counsel yourself with care: Satie *Gnossienne* (3)

conservant (Fr.) keeping: Deb. *Ch.Corner* (5) **— le rhythme**

contemplatif (Fr.) contemplative, pensive: Scriabin Prél.Op.74(2)

contenue (Fr.) restrained, suppressed: Scriabin Son.Op.62 **avec un chaleur —**, with a contained warmth

contraire (Fr.) contrary, headstrong: Messiaen *VR6*

contrario (It.) contrary motion: Brahms Var.Op.21(1) **canone in moto —**, canon in contrary motion

contre-sujet (Fr.) counter-subject, the second subject in a fugal piece

copla (Sp.) stanza, ballad: Gran. *Goy.*(2); Albéniz Op.47(4)

coquetterie (Fr.) coquetry, flirtatiousness: Liszt *Apparitions* (2) **avec —**

cor (Fr.) horn

corneille (Fr.) crow

cornemuse (Fr.) bagpipe

corona (It.) the pause-mark, 'crown': Dvořák Op.101(6)

corrander (Sp.) Spanish dance, courante

corrente (It.) running, flowing: Schum. *Abegg Var.*(3)

couchant (Fr.) sunset

coulé (Fr.) running, flowing: Messiaen *FdJ*

courante (Fr.) dance of varying form in France and Italy, but usually flowing in triple time, and starting near the end of a bar

courez (Fr.) run: Satie *le Traîneau*

crèche (Fr.) manger, crib: Messiaen *VR16*

crescendo (It.) increasing, growing, in tone/volume, getting louder

cri (Fr.) cry: Scriabin Prél.Op.74(3) comme un —
criard (Fr.) shrill: Messiaen VR16
criblé (Fr.) sifted, filtered: Satie Noct.(3)
cristallin (Fr.) crystalline, jewel-like, gem-like: Scriabin *Poème*
    Op.61 —, perlè, jewelled set with pearls; Son.Op.70
croisées (Fr.) crossed
croisez (Fr.) cross hands: Poulenc *Impromptu*
croix (Fr.) cross
crotales (Fr.) antique cymbals
Csardas (Hung.) Hungarian national dance in contrasted moods,
    often with a slow introduction
cuisses (Fr.) thighs: Satie *Le Piège de Méduse*
cuivré (Fr.) copper, brassy: Messiaen VR10
cupamente (It.) darkening, becoming sombre
cupo (It.) dark: Janăćek *Auf Verwachsenen Pfade* (10)
cygne (Fr.) swan
cyprés (Fr.) cypress trees

——D——

da (It.) from
D.C. (It.) da Capo, from the beginning. This is the usual ending
    for a Trio, indicating to play its minuet or scherzo again
dahinhüschend (Ger.) hurrying, hastening there; Schollum 7
    Fantasies ziemlich rasch, —, rather fast, hurrying on
da lontano (It.) from afar: Prok. Son.Op.103(4)
Dampfer (Ger.) damper, mute: *see* una corda, soft pedal
Dämpfung (Ger.) damping, muting: Scho. Op.11(1) mit — und
    Pedal, with both 'soft' and sustaining pedals. *See* céleste
dans (Fr.) in, with: Satie *Gnossienne* (2), — une grande bonté,
    with great generosity; Satie *Gnossienne* (6) — une saine
    supériorité, with a healthy superiority
dansant (Fr.) dancing: Deb. *Études* (7)
danseuse (Fr.) female dancer
danzando (It.) dancing: Medtner Op.55(1) allegro —
d'après un air de 'La Gazzaladra', (Fr.) after a tune from *The*
    Thieving Magpie (Rossini); Chopin *Pol.B min.*posth.

Daumen (Ger.) thumbs

débordante (Fr.) overflowing, bursting banks

début (Fr.) beginning

déchirant (Fr.) tearing: Scriabin Prél.Op.74(1)

décidé (Fr.) decisive: Ravel *Menuet Antique*; Albéniz *Iberia*; Poulenc *Suite* (1920)

deciso (It.) decisive, resolute: Liszt*; Gran. *Goy.*(5)

declamato (It.) declaimed, standing out: Liszt *Don Giovanni*; Busoni *Fanta. Contrappuntistica*

decresc(endo) (It.) growing less, reducing in volume

défunt (Fr.) dead, having died

dehors (Fr.) *see* **en** —

delentando (It. - apparently a coinage) slowing down: Schub. Son.D566

del(l)iberando (It.) with deliberation, thought: Clementi Son.Op.50(3) — **e meditando**

délicat (Fr.) delicate: Deb. *Epitaph* (6)

delicatament(e) (Fr., It.) delicately: Brahms, Chopin, Clementi, Deb., Liszt*

delicatezza (It.) delicacy: Liszt trs. Schub. 'Auf dem Wasser' **con** —, delicately; Mouss. *Pict.*(1); Schub. Son.B flat (1823)(3) **allegro vivace con** —, Scriabin, *Feuillet* Op.58

delicatissimo (It.) with great delicacy: Field Noct.4, 8; Chopin*

delicato (It.) delicately: Chopin *Études* Op.10(7); Schum. Son.Op.11(1)

delirando (It.) delirious, frenzied: Liszt *12 Grandes Études* (10) **vibrante** —

délire (Fr.) delirium: Scriabin Son.Op.64

delizio (It.) delight: Scriabin Son.Op.53(1), Prél.Op.48(2) **con** —, with delight, deliciously

dérante (Fr.) delirious, frenzied: Scriabin Son.Op.62

derniérement (Fr.) lastly: Satie *Pièces Froides*

désespoir (Fr.) despair, hopelessness: Satie, title

désordonné (Fr.) untidy, uncoordinated: Scriabin Poème Op.72(2)

dessous (Fr.) under, beneath: Deb. *Images* (1) **commencer un peu au** — **du mouvement**, start a little below the speed for the piece; Poulenc Tocc.

dessus (Fr.) above, treble

destra (It.) right: **la mano** —, the right hand

détaché (Fr.) short (notes): Deb. Prél.1(12) — et rhythmé; Poulenc
    Imp.3; Prok. Son.Op.83(3); Satie *Sonneries de la Rose*
déterminé (Fr.) resolute, decisive: Satie *Les trois Valses*
deutlich (Ger.) clear, distinct
Deutsch (Ger.) German
Deutsches tempo (Ger.) time appropriate for German Dance or
    Länder – moderato; Schub. *Ländler* Op.171
deux pédales (Fr.) with soft and sustaining pedals together: Deb.
    Prél.1(9)
devient (Fr.) becomes: Scriabin Son.Op.62
di (It.) by, from, of
diable à resort (Fr.) jack-in-the-box
Dichter spricht (Ger.) poet speaks: Schum. *Ksz.*(13), title
Didone abbandonata (L.) Dido, Queen of Carthage, committed
    suicide after being abandoned by Aeneas because of his
    duty to travel and found Rome. Clementi called his sonata
    (Op.50(3)) 'scena tragica' after this theme
dieselbe (Ger.) the same: Beeth. Bag.Op.126(6)
Dieu (Fr.) God
dim., diminuendo (It.) diminuer (Fr.) diminishing, getting softer
di nuovo (It.) afresh
disent (Fr.) say: Messiaen *VR*13
disinvolto (It.) easy-going, confident: Medtner Op.26(1) poco
    giocoso —, lightly and easy-going
disperato (It.) recklessly, desperately: Liszt*
distintamente (It.) clearly, well-articulated: Bach/Busoni
    Chaconne; Liszt *12 Grandes Études*(8), *Apparitions*
divertimento (It.) amusement, diversion, suite of that character
divisés (Fr.) divided
divocione (It.) devotion: Liszt *Consolation* (2)
doch (Ger.) then
dol(ce) (It.) sweet: e.g. Albéniz *Iberia* — ma sonoroso; Busoni
    Son'a ad usum infantis — ma marcando; Elgar Op.46 —
    espress; Fauré *Valse-Caprice* Op.30 — tenuto ad espres-
    sivo; Franck Prél. non troppo —; Liszt *A de P*(5) —
    grazioso; *Apparitions*, — parlante; *Don Giovanni* —
    teneramente; *12 Grandes Études* — ma ben marcato ed
    espressivo il canto; Martinů *Puppets* (2); Scriabin, —
    cantabile; Sho. Son.1 Op.12 — ma marcando
dolcemente (It.) sweetly: Gran. *Goy.*(6)

dolcezza (It.) sweetness: Prok. Son.Op.103(1) **con una — espressiva**

dolcissimo (It.) very sweetly: Albéuiz, Barber, Brahms, Chopin*, Fauré, Field, Franck, Grieg, Ireland, Janáček, Liszt*, Prok., Scriabin, Tch.; Liszt *A de P* (1) **— equalmente**; trs. Schub. 'Ave Maria' **gli accompagnamenti sempre —**; *Soir* (4) **— placido**; *A de P* (2) **— e armonioso**; *Gondoliera* **— e tranquillo**; *12 Grandes Études* (3) **— legato cantando**; *EET* (9) **— capricciosamente**

dolente (It.) sad, mournful: Bach/Busoni, Chopin, Janáček, Liszt*, Medtner; Beeth. Son.Op.110(3) **arioso —**, sad song; Clementi Son.Op.50(3) **adagio —**; Liszt *Fanta*.Op.2, **— perdendosi**; *A de P3* **espressivo —**

dolore (It.) sadness: Mouss. *Pict*.(2, 6) **con —**, sadly, mournfully; Liszt *Fanta*. Op.2 **recitando — ma semplice**, recited sadly but simply; Prok. Son.Op.103(1) **con una — espressiva**

doloroso (It.) mournful, sad: Gran. *Goy*.(4,5); Liszt *Canzone, A de P3*; Scriabin, Prél.Op.16(6), Maz.Op.3(5), Son.Op.23(3); Tch. Op.37a **andante — e molto cantabile**, mournfully, at moderate speed and very songfully

donnaire (Sp.) with charm, grace

Doppelgriffen (Ger.) double notes (i.e. with one hand)

doppio movimento (It.) twice as fast as before

doré (Fr.) gilded: Messiaen *F d J* **—, les accents très marquées**

Dorf (Ger.) village

dormant (Fr.) dormant, sleeping

dort (Fr.) sleeps

double (Fr.) a) double, repeated note or part: Deb. *PP* **le — plus lent**, the repetition slower; b) a musical variation of a theme, doubling the speed

douce (Fr.) sweet, gentle: Satie *Les Fils des Étoiles* **— demande**, gentle question. *See also* **doux**

doucement (Fr.) sweetly: Deb. *Images*2(1), **— sonore**; *Epitaph* 3, **— en dehors**, prominent but sweet; Poulenc **— expressif** *Nocturne* 6

douceur (Fr.) sweetness: Scriabin *Poème* Op.63(2) **une fausse —**, a false sweetness; Son.Op.64 **avec une profonde —**; Son.Op.68 **avec une — de plus en plus caressant et empoisonnée**, with a sweetness more and more embracing and poisonous

douloureux/se (Fr.) mournful, sad: Deb. Prél.1(6); Satie *Gymnopédie* (1); Scriabin Prél.Op.74(1); Son.Op.70 **un volupte** —, a gloomy pleasure

doux (Fr.) sweet: e.g. Deb. *Ch.Corner* — **et un peu gauche**, sweet and slightly gauche; — **et estompé**, sweet and blurred; Messiaen *VR5* — **et mystérieux**; Ravel, *Pavane* **assez** —, **mais d'une sonorité large**, fairly sweet but with a full tone

dr(oit) Fr.) right (hand)

Drachentanz (Ger.) dragon dance

dram(m)atica (It.) dramatically, theatrically: Gran. *Goy**; Liszt *Don Giovanni*; Scriabin Prél.Op.76(1), Son.Op.23

drängend (Ger.) pressing on, hurrying: Scho. Op.33(6), Op.11(3)

Dreiklängen (Ger.) chords of three notes, triads

dringend (Ger.) urgent, pressing on; Schum. *Non.* Op.21(4)

D.S. (It.) **dal Segno** from the Sign

du bout de la pensée (Fr.) 'from the tip of the thought': Satie *Gnossienne* (1)

du coin de la main (Fr.) with the corner (i.e. edge) of the hand: Satie, *Danses de Travers*

Dudelsack (Ger.) bagpipe

due (It.) two, — **volti**, twice: — **corde**, two strings (use 'soft' pedal); Mn *SWW*(32) as two equal parts: Liszt *Robert le Diable* — **temi marcato**, both themes stressed

duetto (It.) duet: Mn *SWW*(18)

dumka Slovakian dance alternating lively and elegiac moods

dur (Ger.) major: — Beeth. Prel.Op.89 — **Tonarten** major keys

dur (Fr.) hard: Satie *Le piège de Méduse* — **comme le Diable**, hard as the Devil

durchaus (Ger.) throughout

durées (Fr.) (durations) epochs, ages: Messiaen *VR6*

dureté (Fr.) hardness: Deb. Prél.1(10) **sonore sans** —, resonant, but not hard; Deb. *Images* (1)

durezza (It.) hardness: Janáček *Predtucha* (1905) **con** —, with hard tone

E

e(d) (It.) and

ebrezza (It.) intoxication: Scriabin Son.Op.53 **con una — fantastica**, with a fantastic sense of drunkenness

Ecossaise(n) (Fr., Ger.), fairly fast dance in 2/4 time, popularly regarded as Scottish in origin: Beeth. Chopin, Schub.

échange (Fr.) change, incarnation

écho (Fr.) echo: Deb. Prél.1 **comm un — de la phrase entendue précédément**, like an echo of the phrase heard previously; Liszt *A de P*1(1)

éclairs (Fr.) flashes of lightning: Scriabin Son.Op.64

éclatant (Fr.) bursting out: Scriabin *Poème* Op.72; Deb. Prél.2(12); Poulenc *Suite* (2), **le chant —**, the tune bursting out, resounding

ecstasi (It.) ecstasy

effacent (Fr.) effacing: Deb. Prél.2(1) **en retendant et en s' —**, slowing down as it recedes

effetto (It.) effect: Prok. Son.3(1) **con —**, with effect, exaggerated

effleuré (Fr.) touched lightly, brushed: Deb. *Epitaph* 2

effleurer (Fr.) brush, touch lightly: Albéniz *Iberia* **— la note, la laissent vibrer**, just brush the note enough for it to sound

effrondement (Fr.) collapse, break-up: Scriabin Son.Op.62

ég(u)alemente (Fr., It.) equally, evenly, 'legato': Liszt*, Bach/Busoni *Chaconne*; *Son'a ad usum infantis*; Deb. *Études* 5 **très — rhythmé, sans presser**, with very regular rhythm and without hurrying

ég(u)al (Fr.) equal, regular: Deb., Ravel, Schum.; Deb. Prèl.2(12) **et lointain**, even and distant; *Epitaph* 6 **extrèmement doux et —**; Ravel *Gaspard* **bien — de sonorité**, very even in sound; Strav. Son.(1924)(1) **legatissimo e molto —**

église (Fr.) church: Tch. Op.39(22)

Ehestift (Ger.) (love-)match, engagement

eigens (Ger.) (own) specifically

eilen (Ger.) to hurry; Bach/Busoni *Chaconne* **non —**; Liszt *12 Grandes Études* (6) **nicht —**

einfach (Ger.) simple

einig (Ger.) (one) any, some
einsam(er) (Ger.) lonely
einschlummern (Ger.) fall asleep; Schum. *Ksz.*(12)
Einzelstimme (Ger.) single voice, part
élan (Fr.) bound, spring: Scriabin Son.Op.70 **avec — lumineux, vibrant**, with a luminous, vibrant spring
élargi (Fr.) broadened: Deb. Prél.2(12) **mouvement —**
elegante (It.) elegant
elegantemente (It.) elegantly: Liszt Pol.2, *Apparitions* 3; Busoni Son. **allegretto —**; Chopin, Var.posth.
eleganza (It.) elegance: Liszt *Valse Oubliée* (2), *HR*10; Prok. Op.20(6) **con —**, elegantly
elevatione, elevato (It.) height: Prok. Son.3(1) **con —**, loftily
élégance (Fr.) elegance: Deb. *PP*(2) **avec une — grave et lente**, with a grave, slow elegance
éliminé à droit (Fr.) drop out to the right (the left hand part is transferred to the right hand): Messiaen *VR*6
éliminé à gauche (Fr.) drop out to the left (the right hand part is transferred to the left hand): Messiaen *VR*6
éloignant (Fr.) distancing, removing: Deb. *Masques* **sourd et en s' —**, dull and fading far away; Prél.1(9)
émotion (Fr.) emotion, feeling: Deb. *Ch.Corner* (6) **avec une grande —**, with great feeling; Messiaen *Les sons Impalpable de Rêve*
Empfindung (Ger.) feeling: Beeth. Son.Op.90; Mn Op7(1); Beeth. Son.Op.101 **mit innigsten —** with deepest feeling (also Son.Op.109(3)); Schum. *Alb.Y.* **mit inniger —**, with inward feeling, introspection
empfindungsvoll (Ger.) full of feeling: Schum. Op.126(5)
empoisonné (Fr.) poisoned: Scriabin Son.Op.68 **avec un douceur de plus en plus caressant et —**, with a sweetness more and more caressing and poisonous
emporté (Fr.) excited, carried away: Deb. Prél.1(2) *Études*5
ému (Fr.) moved, touched: Messiaen *Instants Défunts*
en (Fr.) in, while
enamorados (Sp.) lovesick
enchantement (Fr.) enchantment, magic: Scriabin Son.Op.62
encore (Fr.) again
Ende (Ger.) end
en décire (Fr.) raving, delirious: Scriabin Son.Op.64

en dehors (Fr.) outside, prominent, standing out: e.g. Deb.
Epitaph 4 doucement —, prominent but sweet; Poulenc,
Imp.4 très —; Ravel *Gaspard* un peu — mais sans expres-
sion, standing out a little but without expression

energia (It.) energy: Schum. *Ét.Symp.*Op.13(3) con —, energetically; *Fasch.* (4) con molto —; *Fant.*Op.67 maestoso con —,
majestically with energy

energico (It.) with vigour: Barber, Beeth., Brahms, Chopin,
Janáček, Liszt, Mn, Weber; Brahms Son.Op.2 allegro non
troppo ma —; Gran. *Goy.*(6) — con ritmo, with vigour and
rhythm; Liszt *12 Grandes Études* (3) — vibrante; *Fanta.*
Op.2 — con fuoco; *EET*(5) — con bravura; *EETF*(4) con
bravura molto —; *3 Concert Studies* (1) — appassianato
assai; HR marcato —; *Apparitions* (3) sempre strepitoso —
, constantly noisy and energetic

Energie (Ger.) energy: Bach/Busoni *Chaconne* mit rhythmischer —

energique (Fr.) with energy: Messiaen *VR* 16

energisch (Ger.) energetic, vigorous: Schum. *BB*(10)

enfouissez le son (Fr.) muffle the sound: Satie *Gnossienne* (3). *See
also* Céleste

énigmatique (Fr.) enigmatic: Scriabin *Poème* Op.63(1)

enlevez (Fr.) raise

enlargissant (Fr.) broadening, 'allargando': Ravel *Menuet
Antique*

ennuyée (Fr.) bored, restless: Satie *Le Tango* modére et très —

en retenant (Fr.) holding back, withheld: Ravel *Valses Nobles* très
expressif et —, very expressive and lingering

Enschlossenheit (Ger.) resolution, decisiveness: Beeth.
Son.Op.101(3)

en se regardant de loin (Fr.) looking at each other from a
distance: Satie *Le Fils des Étoiles*

enthousiasme (Fr.) enthusiasm, fervour: Scriabin Op.71(2)

entraîner (Fr.) to drag along: Scriabin Son.Op.62

entrechoquent (Fr.) clash, collide: Bartók *Mikro.* 110

entschwundene Tage (Ger.) lost, vanished days

envelopé(e) (Fr.) enveloped, wrapped, muffled, shrouded:
Messiaen *La Colombe* d'une sonorité très — de pédales,
much overlaid by the pedals

en y regardant à deux fois (Fr.) on looking at it twice: Satie
Danses de Travers

épanouissement (Fr.) opening up, spreading: Scriabin Son.Op.62
— de force mystérieux

épouvantable (Fr.) terrible: Messiaen VR18

épouvante (Fr.) terror: Scriabin Son.Op.62 — surgit, the terror
rises

equale (It.) equal, level: Busoni *Fanta.Son.* — e dolce fliessend,
flowing evenly and sweetly

équivaut (Fr.) equivalent

erleichert (Ger.) simplified, easier

ermattert (Ger.) tired out, exhausted: Beeth. Son.Op.110(3)

ernst (Ger.) earnest, serious

Ernteliedchen (Ger.) little harvest song: Schum *Alb.Y.*(24)

eroico (Ger.) heroic: Liszt *Fanta.on 'Rienzi'*; *Sunt Lacrimae
Rerum*, *HR*14, *A de P*35

erregt (Ger.) agitated, stirred up: Schollum 7 *Fantasies*

Errinerung (Ger.) memory, recollection, reminiscence: Schum.
Alb.Y.(28), title

erschienen (Ger.) appeared, was published

erste(s) (Ger.) first

esaltatione (It.) exaltation, excitement: Liszt trs. Schub. 'Sei mir
gegrüsst' con —, excitedly

esaltato (It.) exalted, lofty, grand: Scriabin *Études* Op.42(6);
Son.Op.53 presto tumultuoso —, very fast, stormy and lofty

escenas (Sp.) scenes

espansione (It.) breadth, expansion: Barber *Galop* Op.28; Liszt
Op.7; Gran. *Goy.*(2) — appassionata; Ireland Son.(2) con
—

espectro (Sp.) spectre, ghost: Gran. *Goy.*(6) serenata del —, serenade of the spectre

espressione (It.) *see* expressione

espress(ivo) (It.) with expression, with feeling: Bartók, Beeth.*,
Berg, Brahms*, Chopin, Clementi, Dvořák, Fauré, Elgar,
Field, Franck, Gran., Haydn, Ireland, Janáček, Liszt*,
Medtner; Mn*, Prok., Rach., Sho., Strav., Tch.; Beeth.
Son.Op.101(1) — e simplice; Field, Noct.11 molto — e
languido; Gran. *Goy*(6) — ad lib; *Mephisto* — amoroso;
Apparitions — piangendo, plaintively expressive; Prok.
Son.Op.83(1) — e dolente. *See also* expressivo

esquisses (Fr.) sketches, drafts, rough versions: Satie, title; Deb.,
title, 'D'un Cahier d' —', from a book of sketches, title

éstampes

éstampes (Fr.) prints, engravings: Debussy, title
estinto (It.) extinguished: Liszt *12 Grandes Études* (3) *EET* (2)
estompé (Fr.) blurred: Albéniz *Iberia*; Deb. *Ch.Corner*(4) **doux et
—**, sweet and blurred; Poulenc Noct.1 **l'accompaniment
très —**, the accompaniment very blurred
éteignant (Fr.) extinguishing: Scriabin Son.Op.70 **s' —**, extinguishing itself
estribillo (Sp.) refrain 'ritornello': Gran. *Danses* (4)
éteinte (Fr.) extinguished, faint: Scriabin Son.Op.70 **une douce
langueur de plus en plus —**, a sweet languor fading away
étincelant (Fr.) sparkling: Scriabin *Études* Op.65(3); Son.Op.64
étoile (Fr.) star: Satie *Le Fils des Étoiles*
étouffe (Fr.) smothered: Deb. *Epitaph* (2)
étrange (Fr.) strange: Scriabin *Morceau* Op.52(2)
étrangeté (Fr.) strangeness: Scriabin *Poème* Op.63(2) **avec une —
subite**, with a sudden strangeness
être plus près (Fr.) be nearer: Satie *Le Fils des Étoiles*
étude (Fr.) study
etwas (Ger.) somewhat, a bit
éviter (Fr.) avoid: Satie *Danses Gothiques*
exaltacio (Sp.) height: Gran. *Esc.Rom*(6) **con — poetica** loftily
poetical
exaltation (Fr.) exaltation, elation: Scriabin Son.Op.70 **avec une
joyeuse —**, with a joyful elation
exalté (Fr.) exalted, lofty: Satie *Le Golf*
express(if) (Fr.) expressively, with feeling: Albéniz, Deb.*,
Messiaen, Poulenc; Deb. Prél.1(8, 16), 2(5) **très calme et
doucement —**, very calmly and with feeling; Prel.1(10) **—
et concentré**; Prél.2(10) **très doux et très —**; *Ch.Corner*,
délicatement —; *Epitaph* 5 **librement —**; Poulenc Noct.(2)
très —
expression, avec expression (Fr.) (with) feeling: Satie *Gnossienne*
(6)
expressione (It.) expression: Beeth.*, Brahms, Chopin, Clementi,
Field, Franck, Haydn, Kuhlau, Liszt, Mouss., Prok. **con —**;
Bartók *Mikro.* **tutte le due voci con molta —**, both parts
with great expression; Beeth. Son.Op.31(1), (2) **— e
semplice**, with expression and simply; Bag.Op.33(6) **con
una certa — parlente**, with a certain speaking expression;
Brahms Son.Op.5 **con molto —**; Mouss. *Pict.*(2) **senza —**,

38

without expression; Prok. Son.4(2) **con una dolce** —, with a sweet expression; Franck *Prél., Aria, Finale* **tutta** —, with all expression

expressivamente (It.) very expressively, with much expression, with great feeling: Albéniz, Beeth., Brahms, Clementi*, Mn*, Satie, Schum.*, Scriabin*; Schum. Son.Op.11(1) **senza passione, ma** —, without passion, but with expression

expressivo (It.) expressively: Brahms Ball.(1) Op.10 — **e dolce**

extase (Fr.) ecstasy

extasis (Sp.) ecstasy: Gran. *Esc.Rom.*(2) **con** —, ecstatically

extatique (Fr.) ecstatic: Messiaen *VR*19; Scriabin Son.Op.64 **avec une volupté radieuse,** —, with a radiant, ecstatic pleasure

—— **F** ——

F(FFF), forte, fortissimo (It.) loud, very loud: Albéniz *Iberia* 'El Puerto' **ffff plus fort encore si possible**; Rach. *MM* Op.16(4, 6) **ffff**

Fabel (Ger.) fable: Schum. *Fant.*Op.12

facheux (Fr.) annoying: Satie *Facheux Exemple*

facile (It, Fr.) simple, easy: **ossia più** —, simpler alternative

façon (Fr.) style, manner

faites (Fr.) make, cause to: Deb. *Images* (2) — **vibrer**, make vibrate

fandango (Sp.) argument, row, tiff: Gran. *Goy.*(3), title, '— **by Lamplight**'

fantasia (It., Fr., Ger., Sp.) fantasy, imagination, fantasy piece: Gran. *Goy.*(4) **con molto** —

fantasque (Fr.) whimsical: Deb. *Masques* **tres vif et** —

fantasticamente (It.) fantastically: Liszt *EETF*(6)

fantastico (It.) fantastically: Scriabin *Études* Op.53(1), Op.65(1)

fantastique (Fr.) fantastic: Scriabin Op.71(1)

fantôme (Fr.) phantom

Faschingsschwank (Ger.) carnival jest, prank: Schum. Op.26, title

Faschingsnacht (Ger.) carnival night: Schum. Op.2, title

fast (Ger.) almost

fastoso (It.) festive, sumptuous, splendid: Scriabin *Poème* Op.34

faussaires (Fr.) forgers, *see* ivrognes

fausse (Fr.) false: Scriabin *Poème* Op.63(2) **avec une — douceur,** with a false sweetness

fauvette (Fr.) warbler, warbling, birdsong: Messiaen , title, 'La — les jardins'

feierlich (Ger.) solemn, as a ceremony: Bach/Busoni *Chaconne,* **— gemessen, doch night schleppend,** with dignified movement, but not dragging

felicita (It.) joy: Gran. *Goy.(5)* **come una — nel dolore,** like a joy without pain

fermamente (It.) firmly, decisively: Busoni, *Fanta. Contrappuntistica*; Scriabin Prél.Op.39(1)

Fermata(e) (Ger., It.) pause(s): Schollum *7 Fantasies* (3), **sehr lange —,** very long pause

fermezza (It,) firmness: Medtner Op.11(1) **con —** firmly

fermo (It.) still, fixed: Gran. *Goy.(5)* **— e a tempo,** strictly in time

Fern(e) (Ger.) far, distant: Schum. *Davidsbündler* **wie aus der —,** as from afar: *Nov.*Op.21(7) **Stimme aus der —,** voice from afar

feroce (It.) ferociously, fiercely: Brahms, Dvořák, Janáček, Liszt, Mouss., Prok.

fest (Ger.) firm, strict: Bach/Busoni *Chaconne*

festivamente (Ger.) festively: Scriabin Prél. Op.48(4), Op.34

festlich (Ger.) festive: Schum. *Nov.*Op.21(4) **rauschend und —,** noisy and festive

feuille(s) (Fr.) leaf (leaves), page(s): **— d'album,** page from an album; Deb. *Images* (2) **cloche à travers les —,** bells over leaves

feuillet d'album (Fr.) little piece from an album (*cf* **Albumblatt**): Scriabin *Morceau* Op.45(1), Op.58; Tch. Op.19(3)

feurig (Ger.) fiery: Brahms *Scherzo* Op.4; Liszt trs. *Lohengrin*; Mn Op.3 **kräftig und —,** strongly and with fire

feux follets (Fr.) will o' the wisps: Liszt *EET(5)*

fiducia (It.) honesty: Scriabin *Poème* Op.72(2) **con —,** sincerely, honestly

fièrement (Fr.) proudly: Deb. *Berceuse Hèroique*

fiero (It.) proudly: Scriabin Prél. Op.37(2), 48(1),74(5)

fils (Fr.) son: Satie (title), 'Le — des Étoiles', The Son of the

Stars; Messiaen *VR5*

fin (Fr.) end; (It.) until

finir (Fr.) finish: Satie *Le Fils des Étoiles*

finezza (It.) finesse, delicacy: Scriabin *Morceau* Op.49(3) **con** —; delicately

fino (It.) until

flamme (Fr.) flame, fire: Scriabin *Poème* Op.72

flauto (It.) flute: Busoni *Fanta. Contrappuntistica*

flebile (It.) feeble, faint: Liszt Fanta. Op.2, *HR*13

Fliege (Ger.) fly (noun)

fliessend(er) (Ger.) flowing, more flowing: Scho. Op.11 (1, 2); Schollum 7 *Fantasies* (4, 7) — **bis rasch**, flowing until fast; Webern Op.27, **ruhig** —, flowing quietly

flottande (Fr.) floating: Deb. *Cahier* **la basse toujours un peu** —, the bass always slightly floating

flottant (Fr.) floating, light: Deb. Prél.1.(4), (10) — **et sourd**, floating and muffled

flüchtig (Ger.) (flighty) slight, whimsical, fleeting: Scho. Op.19(1)

focosamente (It.) fierily: Scriabin Son.Op.30(2)

fois (Fr.) times: Liszt trs. *Trovatore* **Pédale 4** — **à chaque mésure**, pedal 4 times in each bar

foissonnement (Fr.) abundance: Messiaen *VR6*

folies (Fr.) follies, madnesses

fond (Fr.) bottom: Satie *Pièces Froides*

fondu (Fr.) melted, molten: Poulenc *Suite* (2) **très** —, Ravel *Gaspard* (3) **très** — **et bien égal de sonorité**, very liquid and even in sound; *Miroirs* (3) **un trémolo très** —, a very fluid tremolo

forte (It.) strong, loud, *see* f: Chopin Ball.Op.23, Liszt, trs. *Norma* **il piu** — **possible**, as loud as possible

fortissimo (It.) very loud, *see* f

Fortsetzung (Ger.) continuation

forza (It.) force, strength: Brahms, Chopin*, Deb., Liszt*, Mn, Mouss., Schum., Scriabin, **con** —; Brahms, Cadenza Beeth. C min. Conc. **con gran** —; Chopin Noct.Op.48(1) **con tutta la** —, with all strength, as strongly as possible; Elgar Op.10(1) **tutta** —; Franck Ball.Op.9 **con molta** —; Gottschalk *Bamboula* **tutta la** — **possible**; Lizst *EETF* **colla più gran** — **e prestezza**; Pol.(2) **con tutta** —; Ball.(1) **con** —

41

e bravura; Mn *SWW*(10) **sempre con — assai**

forzando (It.) getting louder

foudre (Fr.) thunderbolt, lightning: Messiaen *VR6*

fractionnement (Fr.) splitting, spreading: Messiaen *VR6* — **des accords,** with the chords spread

Frage (Ger.) question

fragile (Fr.) fragile, delicate: Scriabin *Poème* Op.69(1) **gracieux, —**

franc (Fr.) free, open-hearted, candid: Ravel *Valses Nobles* (1)

frappez (Fr.) strike: Deb. *Images* — **les accords sans lourdeur,** strike the chords without heaviness

frei (Ger.) free

freier (Ger.) more freely: Bach/Busoni *Chaconne* **etwas —, doch stets mit rhythmischer Energie,** somewhat more freely but still with strong rhythm

fremder (Ger.) strange: Schum. *Alb.Y.*(29)

frémissant (Fr.) vibrating, quivering: Scriabin Son.Op.70 — **, ailé,** on quivering wings

frescamente (It.) fresh: Medtner Op.26(1)

Freude (Ger.) joy

frisch (Ger.) fresh, lively: Schum. *Alb.Y.*(7, 10) — **und frölich,** fresh and happy; (17) — **und kräftig,** fresh and forceful; *BB*(3)

fröhlich (Ger.) happy, cheerful: Schum. *Alb.Y.*(7)

froid (Fr.) cold: Satie *Pièces Froides*

Frühe (Ger.) morning

früher (Ger.) earlier: **wie —,** as before

Frühling (Ger.) Spring

Frühlingsgesang (Ger.) Spring song: Schum. *Alb.Y.*(15), title

fuga (It.) *see* **fugue**

fughetta (It.) a diminutive fugue or short piece in fugal style, *see* **fugue**

fugue (Fr.) A fugue is a contrapuntal composition, usually with firm structure and tonality, in which an opening subject is taken up by a number of 'voices' or 'parts' in turn. There were many established devices for elaborating the simple basic material, whilst the first and successive parts were occupied with a counter-subject. However, the word means 'flight' or 'fancy', and fugues vary from the strict (using little material not found in the subjects, and working through a seemingly inevitable sequence of keys to a climax in the tonic), to pieces of the same contrapuntal nature but more widely-ranging ideas and less symmetrical shape. Fugue is a technical challenge to the composer as much as is Sonnet or Villanelle to the poet, and many of the greatest examples depart from the 'rules', forcing energy and imagination through self-imposed limitation. *See also* **Stretto**

fulgurant (Fr.) lightning (adj), flashing: Scriabin Son.Op.64

funèbre (Fr.) funereal, funeral march: Scriabin Son.Op.6(2)

funèraille (Fr.) funeral ceremony: Liszt *HPR*(7)

fuoco (It.) fire

fuocoso (It.) fiery, fierily: Franck Op.5; Liszt trs. Schub. 'Ständchen'; *Tarantella*

fürchtenmachen (Ger.) frightening: Schum. *Ksz.*(11)

furia (It.) rage, fury, violence: Clementi Son.Op.50(3) **con** —; Liszt *Don Giovanni* **presto** —, fast and furious; Scriabin Son.Op.53 **vertiginoso** —, dizzy with fury

furiant (Czech) fast Bohemian dance in triple time

furioso (It.) furiously: e.g. Grieg Ball.Op.24 **molto pesante e** — ... **sostenuto e sempre** —; Liszt *EET*(8) **presto** —; Sho. Prel.Op.34(20) **allegretto** —

Füssen (Ger.) feet

fut (Fr.) was, once existed

fuyant (Fr.) fleeing, fleeting: Deb. Prél.1(11)

——— G ———

g. (Fr.) **gauche**, left hand

gaiement (Fr.) cheerfully, brightly: Chopin Maz.Op.6(2); Satie *Petite Danse, Le Piccadilly*

gallardia (Sp.) gallantry: Gran. *Goy.*(1) **con** —

gallardo (Sp.) Galliard, slow Spanish dance (probably originating in N. Italy in 4/4/ time)

Galop (Ger.) fast dance in duple time, originally German

Gang (Ger.) progress, walk, promenade

gangar (Nw.) a slow-stepping dance in triple time

garbato (It.) with grace, elegance: Liszt *Valse Oubliée* (2)

garbo (It.) grace, elegance

gardez (Fr.) keep: — **la pédale,** keep the pedal down

Gaspard (Fr.) (Caspar) devil: Ravel, title, ' — **de la Nuit**', Devil of the Night

gauche (Fr.) gauche, clumsy, left-handed: Deb. *Ch.Corner* **doux et un peu** —, sweet and a little rough

gavot(te) (Fr.) a slowish French dance in duple time

gazouillement (Fr.) rustling, twittering: Sinding Op.32(3)

g. dessous (Fr.) **gauche dessous,** with left hand below

g. dessus (Fr.) **gauche dessus,** with left hand above

Gebet (Ger.) prayer

gebunden (Ger.) tied together, 'legato': Schum. *Alb.Y.*(22)

gedankenvoll (Ger.) pensive, full of thought

Gedenken (Ger.) memory

Gegenbewegung (Ger.) contrary motion

gegeneinander (Ger.) against each other, opposed

gehalten (Ger.) steady, with control

Geheimnis (Ger.) secret, mystery

Geister (Ger.) ghosts, spirits

geistlich (Ger.) ghostly, spiritual: Grieg Op.17(9)

gekreuzt (Ger.) crossed

gemendo (It.) moaning: Busoni *Fanta. Contrappuntistica*

genug (Ger.) enough, quite

Geräusch (Ger.) noise: Schum. Op.2

gerbe (Fr.) spray of flowers, garland: Messiaen VR1(58)

Gesang hervorgehoben (Ger.) the song made prominent, emphasised: Liszt trs. *Lohengrin*

gesangvoll (Ger.) singing, full of song; Beeth. Son.Op.109(3); Schum. *Alb.Y.*(28), *BB*(6); *Nov.*Op.21(7) **einfach und** —; simple and full of song

Geschichte (Ger.) story: Schum. *Ksz* (2)

geschmeidiges Abheben der Hand (Ger.) smooth, supple raising of the hand: Liszt Fanta.Op.2

geschwind (Ger.) fast, quick: Schum. *BB*(4); Beeth. Son.Op.90(2) **nicht zu — und sehr singbar vorzutragen,** to be taken not too fast and with deep singing tone; Son.Op.101(3) — **doch nicht zu sehr,** fast, but not too fast; Son.Op.110(3) **nach und nach wieder geschwinder,** little by little faster again; Liszt trs. Schub. 'Aufenthalt' **nicht zu —, doch**

kräftig, not too fast, but strongly

gesungen (Ger.) as if sung, **'cantabile'**

geteilte (Ger.) divided, split

getragen (Ger.) (drawn), sustained: Schum. Son.Op.23(3), *BB*(11)

gewidmet (Ger.) dedicated

ghitarra (Sp.) guitar: Albéniz Op.47(4) **come una — il canto** the tune as if on a guitar

gibet (Fr.) gibbet, gallows: Ravel *Gaspard de la Nuit* (2)

gigue (Fr.) jig, a dance in rapid triple time, starting usually on the last beat of the bar: Deb. *Études* (1) **mouvement de —;** Mozart K.574 **Eine Kleine —**

giocandamente (It.) joyful, jocund: Medtner Op.11(1)

giocoso (It.) jokingly: Albéniz, Barber, Brahms, Britten, Deb., Elgar, Fauré, Grieg, Liszt, Medtner, Prok., Scriabin, Tch.; Deb. *Études* (11) **— ... scherzando;** Liszt *Apparitions* (2) **piacevole —,** pleasantly humorous: *Tarantella* **— assai;** *HR*10 **vivacissimo —** extremely lively and witty

gioia (It.) joy, delight: Bartók *Mikro.* (142)

gioja (It.) joy, delight: Liszt *Apparitions* **con —**

giojoso (It.) playfully: Liszt *HR*12

giubiloso (It.) jubilant, joyful: Scriabin Son.Op.30(2)

giusto (It.) just, equal, appropriate, strict (time) Schub.Son. Op.143(1) **allegro —;** Chopin *Pol.Fanta,* Op.61; Tch. Op.37a(2); **tempo —,** e.g. Chopin Imp.Op.51, Waltz Op.64(2); Liszt *12 Grandes Études* (10); Mouss. *Pict.* (Promenade)

glas (Fr.) knell: Gottschalk *Morte!*

gleichmässig (Ger.) (proportionate) even, regular: Liszt trs. *Lohengrin*

gli (It.) the

gliss(ando) (It., Fr.) a single-motioned rapid sliding up or down of a scale of adjacent notes. **'Gliss.'** Is occasionally put against a scale passage which is fully written out and may even be fingered, but it is normally reserved for such a passage where only the top and bottom notes are shown, and the figure is to be played by a single supported digit gliding up or down the keys; Barber, Britten, Deb., Liszt, Medtner, Prok.; Deb. Prél.2 **comme un très leger —,** as a very light gliss.; Schollum 7 *Fantasies* (2) **— Weisse Tasten,** gliss. on white keys

glissant (Fr.) sliding: Albéniz *Iberia* **ppppp et — sur les notes,** absolutely as quietly as possible and sliding over the notes

Glocken (Ger.) bells

Glockengeläute (Ger.) bell ringing, pealing

glück (Ger.) happy

Gnom (Ger.) gnome: Mouss. *Pict.*

Gnomenreigen (Ger.) gnome dance

Gnossienne (Fr.); a piece with suggestions of Gnossos, the Cretan city, where lived Minos of Greek mythology, the wise king and, after death, judge in Hades: Satie, title

Gondellied (Ger.) gondolier song: Mn *SWW*(6,12,29)

Goyescas (Sp.) 'Paintings after Goya': Gran., title

grâce (Fr.) grace, gracefulness: Gran. *Goy*(1) **avec beaucoup de —,** with much gracefulness: Scriabin *Poème* Op.61 **avec une — capricieuse,** with a whimsical grace; Op.72(1) **avec une — languissante,** with a languishing grace; Op.72(2) **avec une — dolente,** with grace and grief

grac/zia (It.) grace: *see* **con —**

gracieusement (Fr.) gracefully: Satie *La Water-Chute*

gracieux (Fr.) graceful

grand (Fr.) big, great

gran(de) (It.) great, much

Grande Serre (Fr.) a French mountain: Messiaen *F d J*

grandezza (It.) (size, magnificence) grandeur, grandiloquence: Chopin Noct.Op.48(2) **con —**

grandioso (It.) grandly, majestically: Brahms, Chopin, Dvořák, Franck, Gran., Grieg, Liszt*

grandissant (Fr.) growing: Deb. Prél.1(10) **dans une expression allant —,** with ever-increasing expression

gratter (Fr.) scratch: Satie *Le Piège de Méduse*

Grätzien (Ger.) of the Graces (three Classical goddesses)

grave (It., Fr.) solemn, slow: Bartók, Beeth., Chopin, Gran., Janáček, Rach., Ravel, Satie, Tch.; Beeth. Var.Op.120 **— e maestoso,** solemn and majestic: Mouss. *Pict.*(6) **— energico,** stately and with strength, (10) **— sempre allargando,** slow and stately, ever broadening

gravità (It.) gravity, seriousness: Albéniz Op.47(4) **con —**

grazia (It.) grace: Beeth., Brahms, Chopin, Gottschalk, Gran., Liszt*, Medtner, Scriabin, Tch. **con —**

graziös (Ger.) graceful: Schum. *Albumb.*(19)

graziosamente (It.) gracefully: Chopin, Pol.G# minor; Liszt *Don Giovanni*

grazioso (It.) gracefully: CPE Bach, Barber, Bartók, Beeth., Brahms, Britten, Chopin, Dvořák, Gottschalk, Grieg, Hindemith, Liszt, Martinů, Medtner, Mn, Saint-Saëns, Strav., Tch.; Brahms Op.119(1) — **e giocoso**, with grace and humour; Liszt trs. Schub. 'Die Forelle' — **senza agitatione**

Grillen (Ger.) whims, flights of fancy: Schum. *Fant.*Op.12, title

grive musicienne (Fr.) song-thrush: *La Faurette des Jardins*

gruppetti (It.) ornament, turn: Deb. Prél.1(12) **les — sur le temps**, the ornaments on the beat

guittara (Sp.) guitar: Deb. Prél.1(9) **quasi —**

gusto (It.) taste; spice or discrimination: Liszt *Soir.*(1) **con —**, tastefully

gut (Ger.) good

Gymnopédie (Fr.) imagined dances for three male choirs at an ancient Spartan festival: Satie, title

---

H

---

habañera (Sp.) slow Cuban dance with dotted duple rhythm, with a strong and often 'grace-noted' first beat: Busoni *Fanta On Carmen*; Deb. Prél.2(3)

haletant (Fr.) panting, gasping

halling (Nw.) a lively Scandinavian dance in duple time

halo (Fr.) halo: Poulenc Noct. **dans un — de pédale**, the pedal forming an aura

Hammerklavier (Ger.) pianoforte: the Hammerklavier was specified by Beethoven for the vast Sonata Op.106, the intimate preceding Op.101, and the late Sonatas, Op.109 and 110. It was his affectionate and patriotic name for the instrument (the piano) whose strings were struck by hammers, rather than (as in the harpsichord) plucked. The piano has more tonal response and sympathy to touch. However, Beethoven owned a number of pianos and this prescription for four Sonatas does not mean that everything else was written for the harpsichord – the first sonatas, for instance, were written for Clavecin (Harpsichord) or Pianoforte

Hanswurst (Ger.) jack-in-the-box

hargneux (Fr.) snarling, cantankerous: Satie *Choral Inappétissant*

harmonie (Fr.) (harmony) accompaniment: Poulenc *Improvisation* (6) — très sèche, the accompaniment very precise

harmonieux (Fr.) harmonious: Deb. Prél.1(4) — et souple, (9) doux et —; Images (1), dans une sonorité — et lointaine, with a harmonious and distant tone

Hasche-Mann (Ger.) the game of 'tag' or 'he': Schum. *Ksz.*(3)

hastig (Ger.) hasty, impetuous: Scho. Op.95; Schum. Hum.Op.20

Hauch (Ger.) breeze, breath: Scho. Op.19(6) wie ein —, like a breeze

haut (Fr.) high: Satie *Le Fils des Étoiles*

hâve de corps (Fr.) haggard in body, worn out: Satie *Gnossienne* (6)

Heft (Ger.) book, volume

heftige (Ger.) violent: Mn Op.7(1) mit — Bewegung, with violent motion; Scho. Op.11(3), Op.23

Heimweh (Ger.) home-sickness

Heldenlied (Ger.) heroes' song: Grieg Op.17(11)

hell (Ger.) bright: Schum. *Nov.*Op.21(7) — und lustig, bright and joyful

hervortretend (Ger.) stepping forward, standing out: Grieg Op.57(3); Hindemith Son.3(1)

hetzen (Ger.) rush, charge: Schollum *Fantasies* 7(6) nicht — !, don't rush!

Hexe (Ger.) witch

hin (Ger.) away, gone

hirondelles (Fr.) swallows

höchst (Ger.) highest, most highly, extremely

Hochzeit (Ger.) wedding

Höhepunkt (Ger.) climax, summit

Hongrois (Fr.) Hungarian

honteux (Fr.) rogues, *see* **irrognes**

hübsch (Ger.) pretty, charming, delicate: Schum. *Alb.Y.*(26)

Hügel (Ger.) hill

Hühnerfüssen (Ger.) hens' legs, stilts: Mouss. *Pict.*(9)

Huldigung (Ger.) homage, oath of allegiance

humo(u)r (Fr.) humour, wit: Schum. *Nov.*Op.21(3, 6);

*Fant.*Op.12 ('Grillen', 'Ende vom Lied')

humore (It.) humour: Medtner Op.1(6) con —

Humoreske (Ger.) (humorous and) diverting piece, of which examples by Dvořák, Grieg and Schum. vary greatly in scope and mood

—— **I** ——

1er. Mouvement (Fr.) **premier mouvement,** in the original time: Deb. *Études* (5); Messiaen *VR6*

il (It.) the

imitando (It.) imitating: Liszt *PF5* — **il Flauto,** like a flute; Schum. Hum.Op.20

imitazione (It.) imitation (at different pitch) i.e. starting like a canon, fugally: Haydn Son. E*b*(1773)(2)

immer (Ger.) always, ever: — **schneller,** faster and faster

impalpable (Fr.) intangible, shadowy: Messiaen *VR* **Les sons —** **de rêve,** half-real sounds from dream

impérieux (Fr.) imperious, commanding: Scriabin Prél.Op.74(5), *Études* Op.65(3)

imperioso (It.) imperiously, with authority: Scriabin Son.Op.53(1)

impeto (It.) drive, pace: Liszt *A de P*2(7) **con —**

impetuoso (It.) impetuously, with haste: Franck, Liszt, Schum., Scriabin

implorando (It.) imploringly, entreatingly: Busoni *Fanta. Contrappuntistica*

importe (Fr.) mean, signify

impromptu (It.) a short piece with improvisatory and often song-like character: Chopin, Fauré, Schub., Schum.

improvisato (It.) improvised: Liszt *12 Grandes Études* (8), *EET*(9) *A de P 27* **quasi —; rubato quasi —;** Busoni *Fanta. Contrappuntistica*

improviso (It.) improvisation: Schum. Son.11(4) **quasi —,** like an improvisation

inaf(f)er(r)ando (It.) mysteriously, elusively: Scriabin *Poème* Op.32(1)

incalzando (It.) (pursuing) getting faster: Ireland *For Remembrance*; Liszt* *12 Grandes Études* (10) **incalcando e stringendo**, getting faster and pressing on

incisif (Fr.) incisive, penetrating: Deb. Prél.1(7), 2(12)

incolore (Fr.) colourless: Poulenc *Mout. Perps.*(1)

indeciso (It.) waveringly, hesitantly: Chopin Noct.Op.9(3)

indugiando (It.) loitering, taking one's time: Busoni *Fanta Contrappuntistica* **intimamente e —**, intimately and without haste

inizio (It.) beginning

innig (Ger.) inwardly, from within, soulfully (a fairly rare directive adopted by late Beethoven and Schumann particularly): Liszt trs. Schum. 'Liebeslieder'; Mn *SWW* (20); Scho. Op.25; Schum. *Davidsbündler* (2); Beeth. Son.Op.101(1), 109(3) **mit der innigsten Empfindung**, with the most inward feeling; Schum. Hum.Op.20 — **(con sentimento)**, inwardly, with feeling; *Fant.*Op.12, *Des Abends* **Sehr — zu spielen**, to be played very inwardly: *Alb.*Y.(27) **mit innigen Ausdruck**, with expression from within; (34) **mit inniger Empfindung**, with inward feeling

Innigkeit (Ger.) inwardness, introspection: Schum. *BB*1

innigst (Ger.) very deeply inward, very soulfully: Liszt *Gretchen*

innocente(mente) (It.) simply, innocently

inquiet (Fr.) unquiet, restless: Dvořák Imp.(1880) **agitato e —**, agitated and restless; Prok. Son.Op.83(1)

in relievo (It.) in relief, standing out: Bartók *Mikro.* (106)

intenso (It.) intense: Bartók *Mikro.* (141, 144)

intérieure (Fr.) internal, inner: Messiaen Prél. **marquez le chant et la voix —**, stress the tune and the internal part

intermède (Fr.) interlude, *see* **intermezzo**

Intermezzo (Ger., It.) interlude. Generic title for short pieces by Brahms and others

intimamente (It.) intimate: Ravel *Valses Nobles* (5)

intime (Fr.) intimate: Ravel *Valses Nobles* (5) **dans un sentiment —**, with intimate feeling

intimement (Fr.) intimacy: Satie *Gnossienne* (2)

intimissimo (It.) very intimate: Brahms Ball.Op.10(4) and Op.79(5) **con — sentimento**, with the most intimate feeling; Liszt *Sonnambula* **con — sentimento**

intimité (Fr.) intimacy: Satie *Gnossienne* (2)

intimo (It.) intimate, *see* **con — sentimento**
invoquer (Fr.) invoke
ira (It.) fury, anger: Medtner Op.1(7)
irato (It.) irate, furious: Scriabin Prél.Op.37(4),49(2)
irisée (Fr.) luminous, radiant: Deb. *Images* 2(1) **comme un buée**
 —, like a luminous mist
ironico (It.) ironically, detachedly: Scriabin *Poème* Op.36
ironique (Fr.) ironical, detached: Deb. Prél.2(3); Poulenc
 Improvisations (8)
irrealmente (It.) unreally: Prok. Op.22(20)
irresoluto (It.) irresolute, wavering: Chopin Noct.Op.55(1);
 Prok. Son.Op.84(3); Medtner Op.11(1) **capriccioso ed —**,
 wayward and wavering
istesso (It.) the same: **l' — tempo**, in the same time
ivre (Fr.) drunk
ivresse (Fr.) intoxication, rapture: Scriabin Son.Op.70
ivrognes (Fr.) drunkards: **—**, Satie *Danses Gothiques* (7)
 honteux, faussaires drunkards, rogues, forgers
iz (Sp.) **izquierdo** with the left hand: Gran. *Danses* (8)

J

Jagd (Ger.) hunt
Jägerliedchen (Ger.) little hunting song: Schum. *Alb.Y.*(7)
jardins (Fr.) gardens: Deb. *Estampes* (3) **— sous la pluie**, gardens
 in the rain
jede (Ger.) each
jeu (Fr.) game
jeux d'eau (Fr.) fountains, cascades
jiogoso (It.) *see* **giocoso**
joie (Fr.) joy: Messiaen *VR*20 **avec une sentiment de — intense**,
 with a feeling of intense joy; Scriabin *Poème* Op.72 **avec
 une — voilée**, with a hidden joy, **avec une — de plus en plus
 tumultueuse**, with a joy more and more riotous;
 Son.Op.64(3) **avec une — débordente**, overflowing with
 joy
Jota Aragonesa (Sp.) Spanish dance from Aragon

joyeusement (Fr.) joyfully: Albéniz *Iberia* 'El Puerto'
joyeux, joyeuse (Fr.) joyful
Juden (Ger.) Jews: Mouss. *Pict.*(66)

——— K ———

Kamin (Ger.) hearth, fireside: Schum. *Ksz.*(8) **Am** —, by the fire-side
keinesweg (Ger.) no way, not at all: Schollum *7 Fantasies* (5) **die Rhythmen nur ungefähr, keineswegs exakt**, the rhythms only approximate, not at all exact
Kind(er/es) (Ger.) child
Kindergesellschaft (Ger.) (child-business) child society, a group of children: Schum. *Son.Op.*118(2)
Kinderszenen (Ger.) scenes from childhood: Schum., title, Op.15
Kirche (Ger.) church: Tch. Op.39(22)
klagend (Ger.) sad, mournful, elegiac: Beeth. *Son.Op.*110(3) **klagender Gesang**, elegy, lamentation: Schum. *Alb.Y.*(9)
kleine (Ger.) little, small: Brahms *Son.Op.*2(1) **ad lib.** — **Noten**, the little notes as you will
Klirren (Ger.) clash, jangle
Knecht (Ger.) knight: Schum. *Alb.Y.*(12)
Kobold (Ger.) goblin
Kraft (Ger.) strength: Schum. *Imp.Op.*5(8) **mit grosser** —, with great power
kräftig (Ger.) strong, forceful: Liszt trs. Schub. 'Aufenthalt'; Schum. *Nov.Op.*21(1) *Alb.Y.*(17, 29, 31), Op.111(3); Mn Op.7(2) — **und feurig** strongly and with fire
krank (Ger.) ill, sick: Tch. Op.39(23)
Kreisleriana (Ger.) 'All about Kreisler' (an imaginary composer created by E.T.A. Hoffmann many years before the historical violinist and composer, Fritz Kreisler): Schum., title Op.16
Kriegslied (Ger.) battle song: Schum. *Alb.Y.*(31)
Kuhreigen (Ger.) cowherds' dance
kurz (Ger.) short, staccato

kürzer (Ger.) shorter form: Liszt *HR* — **zum Zeichen**, shorter, on
to sign

lac (Fr.) lake
lacrymae (L.) tears: Liszt, title, '**Sunt — Rerum**', 'There are tears
for the nature of things' a quotation, from Virgil's 'Aeneid',
on the tragic elements of life
Lagenwechsel (Ger.) change of position
lagrimoso (It.) tearfully: Liszt *HPR*(7, 9), *A de P*2(7)
laissez vibrer (Fr.) allow to vibrate, 'half-pedal': Deb. *Images* (1);
Rach. Op.42(7)
l'Allemande (Fr.) the German: à —, in the German style, *see*
Allemande
lamentando (It.) lamenting: Clementi Son.Op.50(3)
lamento (It.) lamentation, grief: Mouss. *Pict*(8) con —
lamentoso (It.) mournfully: e.g. Beeth., Schub., Schum.; Liszt
HPR(4), *A de P*27
Ländler (Ger.) German waltz dance(s) in triple time, fairly slow:
Beeth. Schub., Schum.
ländlich (Ger.) of the country, rustic: Schum. *Alb.Y.*(20)
ländlicher (Ger.) rural, pastoral
Landmann (Ger.) peasant: Schum. *Alb.Y.*(10)
langoureux (Fr.) languorous, languid: Albéniz *Iberia* 'El Puerto';
Satie *Poudre d'Or*
langsam(er) (Ger.) slow(er): Scho.Op.23 **allmählich — werden**,
becoming slower and slower
languente (It.) languishing: Busoni *Fanta. on Carmen*: Clementi
Son.Op.50(3); Liszt *Liebesträume* (1), *3 Concert Studies*
langueur (Fr.) languor, listlessness: Scriabin *Morceau* Op.52(1),
Poème Op.61; Son.Op.68 **avec une — naissante**, as a listlessness is born; Son.Op.70 **avec une douce — de plus en
plus éteinte**, with a gentle languor more and more faint
languidamente (It.) languidly: Chopin Noct.Op.62(1)
languide (Fr.) languid: Scriabin *Poème* Op.61

languido (It.) languidly, languishing: Bach/Busoni, Chopin, Clementi, Medtner, Scriabin*; Chopin Noct.Op.15(3) — e **rubato**; Field Noct.11 **molto expressivo e** —

languissant(e) (Fr.) languishing, fainting: Scriabin Son.Op.66; Ravel *Valses Nobles* (6) **très doux et un peu** —, very sweetly and slightly languishing

largamente (It.) broadly: Bartók, Beeth., Brahms, Chopin, Elgar, Franck, Gran., Ireland, Janáček, Liszt, Medtner, Prok.; Bach/Busoni *Chaconne* — **maestoso**, with broad majesty; Elgar Op.46 — **molto maestoso**; Gran. *Danses* (11) — **como recitativo**, broadly, as a recitative; Liszt *12 Grandes Études* (1) **stringendo ma** —, pressing on, but broadly

largamento (It.) broadly: Medtner Op.55(1) —, **lugubre ma non ritardare**, broadly, gloomily, yet not slowing down

large (Fr.) broad, slow, 'largo'

largement (Fr.) broadly, with breadth

larghetto (It.) less broad and slow than **largo** (of which it is diminutive). Next above **adagio**, next below **largo**

largo (It.) broad and slow: Beeth. Son.Op.2 No.2(2) — **appassianato**, slowly and broadly, with passion; Op.10 No.3(2) — **e mesto**, slowly and sadly; Liszt *12 Grandes Études* (6) — **patetico**, slowly and with pathos

larmes (Fr.) tears

las (Fr.) tired: Poulenc Noct.4 **lent, très** —, slow, very weary

Laune (Ger.) whim, caprice: R. Strauss Op.9 **mit** —, whimsically

lebendig (Ger.) lively

lebhaft (Ger.) lively

Lebhaftigkeit (Ger.) life, vivacity, vigour: Beeth: Son.Op.90(1); Schum *Albumb.*(1), Op.23(2); Mn Op.7(5)

lecture (Fr.) reading: Liszt 'Dante' Son. **après une** — **de Dante**, after a reading of Dante

legatissimo (It.) (very tightly bound) very smoothly: Britten, Chopin*, Field, Liszt*, Medtner, Mn, Rach., Schum.*; Scriabin; Chopin Son.Op.4(3) — **e smorzando**, very smoothly and dying away; Strav. Son.(1924) — **e molto equale**, very smoothly and evenly

legato (It.) bound together, smooth, without gaps

legendaire (Fr.) like a legend, simple and rounded: Scriabin Son.Op.68

léger (Fr.) light: Deb. *Ch.Corner* (4) — **mais marqué**, light but stressed

legeramente (It.) lightly: Liszt *HR15*; Poulenc Imp.(2)

légèrement (Fr.) lightly

leggere/o (It.) light

legéreté (Fr.) lightness: Deb. *Images* (1) **avec un — fantasque mais précise**, with a lightness fantastic but exact

leggerezza (It.) lightness: Schum. *Kreis.*(8)

leggieramente (It.) lightly; Franck Imp.Op.25(2)

leggierissimo (It.) very lightly: Beeth., Chopin*, Deb., Grieg, Schum.; e.g. Chopin *Études* Op.10(10), Op.25(5); Gran. *Esc.Rom*(2); Liszt *Tarantella*; *12 Grandes Études* (5) — **velocissimo**, with the utmost lightness and speed; Medtner Op.55(1) — **e giocoso**, very light and joyful; Scriabin Son.Op.53 — **rolando**, very light and fleeting

leggiero (It.) lightly: e.g. Beeth., Chopin, Deb., Field; Gran. *Goy*.(1) **molto — il canto ed est le note d'accompagnemento**, very lightly the tune and also the notes of the accompaniment; Liszt trs. *Lucia di Lammamoor* — **harmonioso**

leicht (Ger.) light

leichtlich (Ger.) lightly: Beeth. Bag. Op.119(6) — **vorzutragen**, to play on lightly

leidenschaftlich (Ger.) passionate: Liszt trs. Schum. 'Frühlingsnacht'; Schum. *Fant* Op.17 **durchaus phantastisch und — vorzutragen**, to be played fantastically and with passion throughout

Leid (Ger.) suffering, misery, pain: Schum. *Alb.Y.* title, '**Leides Ahnung**', foreboding of suffering

Leierkasten (Ger.) (lyre box) a form of portable organ: Tch. Op.39

leis(er) (Ger.) soft, gentle: e.g. Brahms, Schum.*, R. Strauss; Schum. *Alb.Y.*(14) **leise und sehr egal zu spielen**, play gently and very evenly

lent (Fr.) slow

lentamente (It.) fairly slow: Gran. *Esc.Rom.*(5); Prok. Op.22(1)

lentement (Fr.) slowly: Gran. *Goy*(3)

lenteur (Fr.) slowness, dragging: Poulenc *Novelette* (1), **modéré sans —**

lentezza (It.) slowness: Liszt *Apparitions* **senza — quasi allegretto**, moderately fast, without dragging; Prok. Op.22(18) con una dolce —, with a sweet slowness

lento (It.) slow: e.g. Britten *Notturno* — tranquillo; Gran. *Esc.Poet*(2) — molto espressivo; Liszt *A de P*2 — placido; Liszt *Canzone* — doloroso

Lerche (Ger.) lark: Tch. Op.39(21)

letzt(e) (Ger.) last

leyenda (Sp.) legend

liberamente (It.) freely: Schum. *Kreis.*(8) i bassi — e con leggerezza, the bass freely and with lightness

liberté (Fr.) freedom: Deb. Prél.1(5) avec la — d'une chanson populaire, with the freedom of a popular song

libitum (L.) *see* ad libitum

libramente (It.) freely: Gran. *Goy.*(2); Poulenc *Promenade* (1939)

librement (Fr.) freely: Deb. Prél.1(9); *Études*(5) — rhythmé, with a free rhythm; Deb. *Epitaph* (5) — expressif

licenze (It.) licence: Beeth. Son.Op.106(4) Fuga ... con alcune —, fugue with some licence (from strict form)

lié (Fr.) (bound) smooth, 'legato': Satie *Prél.Nazaréen*; Poulenc Noct.7

lieb(er) (Ger.) dear: Schum. *Alb.Y.*(13)

Liebe (Ger.) love

Liebesträume (Ger.) Dreams of Love: Liszt, title

Lied (Ger.) song

Lied(chen) (Ger.) (little) song: Schum. *Alb.Y.*(9)

Liegenlassen (Ger.) leaving, forsaking: Schollum 7 *Fantasies* — des Tones, forsaking of tonality

ligato (It.) *see* legato: Beeth. Son.Op.14 No.2(1, 2)

limpide (Fr.) limpid, clear: Scriabin *Poéme* Op.61; Son.Op.68 pur, —

linke (Ger.) with the left hand

l'istesso (It.) the same

lo (It.) the

Lockruf (Ger.) lowing of cattle

loco (It.) place: 'loco' is used to indicate the place where a previous instruction terminates. Often it shows the end of playing an octave (8vo) above or below the written tones, e.g. Liszt, Liebestraum(2)

loco (Sp.) wild, mad: Gran. *Esc.Rom*(5)

loin (Fr.) far: Deb. Prél.2(12) de tré —, from very far away; Deb.

Études(1) de — ... de plus —, from further and further away

lointain (Fr.) distant: Albéniz *Iberia* 'Evocation', 'El Puerto'; Deb.*; Poulenc Noct.(1); Ravel *Valses Nobles* (8), *Miroirs* (2), *Pavane*

lontana (It.) distant, remote: Britten *Holiday Diary* (4)

lontano (It.) distant, far away: Ireland *For Remembrance*; Janáček *Auf verwachsenem Pfade* (4) **quasi** —

loriot (Fr.) golden oriole: Messiaen *FdJ*

lourdement (Fr.) heavily: Gottschalk *Le Bananier*

lourdeur (Fr.) heaviness: Deb. Prél.1(8), *Études*(12)

Ludus Tonalis (L.) (tonal game). The Play of Notes: Hindemith, title

luftig (Ger.) airy, breezy: Mn Op.7(7)

lugubre (Fr.) doleful, gloomy: Bartók *Mikro.*(141); Grieg Op.65(5) **lento** —; Liszt *Lyon* **sotto voce** —; Medtner Op.55(1) **largamente** —, **ma non ritardare**, broadly and gloomily, but do not slow down

luisant (Fr.) shining, luminous: Satie *Gnossienne* (1)

lumière (Fr.) light

lumineux (Fr.) luminous, bright: Deb. Prél.1(5), *Études*(11); Messiaen *VR5* — **et solennel**; Scriabin *Poème* Op.72; Son.Op.70 — **vibrant**, luminously throbbing

lune (Fr.) moon

lungo/a (It.) long: — **X**, long pause; Bartók *Mikro*(42); Brahms Op.79(2); Chopin Noct.Op.9(3); Liszt *Gretchen*

lusingando (It.) winsomely, flatteringly: Beeth. Son.Op.31 No.3(1); Chopin *Rondeau* Op.5; Deb. *Études* 11; Gran. *Danses* 11; Liszt *Valse Oubliée* (3), *HR8*, *Apparitions*; Medtner Op.26(2)

lustig (Ger.) joyfully, with pleasure, fun: Schum. *Alb.Y.*(9), *Davidsbündler* (13); *Nov*.Op.21(7) **hell und** —, bright and joyful

M

ma (It.) but

Mädchen (Ger.) girl, maid

maesto (It.) majestic: C.P.E. Bach Son.in F

maestoso (It.) majestic, imperious: Beeth., Brahms, Chopin, Elgar, Franck, Gran., Grieg, Ireland, Liszt, Medtner, Mn, Mouss., Rach., Saint-Saëns, Schum., Scriabin, Scho.; Bach/Busoni *Chaconne* **largamente** —, very slow and majestic; Clementi Son.Op.39(2) **adagio** —; Schum *Fant.*Op.17 — **sempre con energie**, majestic and always with energy

maggiore (It.) major (key) as contrasted with minor

Mährisch (Ger.) Moravian

main droit (Fr.) right hand

main gauche (Fr.) left hand

mancando (It.) dying away: Beeth. Son.Op.7(3); Busoni *Fanta. on Carmen*; Chopin Maz.Op.24(3), Pol.Op.26(1); Field Noct.(15); Gran. *Goy.*(4); Liszt *A de P*1(2); trs. Schub. 'Wohin?', trs. Chopin 'Mädchens Wünsch'

mano destro (It.) right hand

mano sinistra (It.) left hand

marcado (Sp.) stressed, marked: Albéniz Op.47(8) **muy** —, very well marked

marcando (It.) being stressed, emphasized: Gran. *Danses* (5)

marcare (It.) mark, stress: Brahms Ball.(4) **senza troppo — la melodia**, do not overstress the tune

marcatissimo (It.) very marked, stressed: Bach/Busoni, Barber, Bartók, Britten, Grieg, Ireland, Liszt*, Lut., Prok., Scho., Scriabin, Sho., Strav.

marcato (It.) stressed, marked: **ben** —, well marked, standing out; e.g. Beeth. Son.Op.106(4) **ben — e tenuto**, stressed and held; Brahms Op.119(4) **sempre pp ma ben** —, very quiet, yet well marked; Sho. Son.Op.12 **dolce ma** —, sweetly, but well marked

marche funèbre (Fr.) funeral march

Märchen (Ger.) fairy tale, legend

marchmässig (Ger.) in march time: Beeth. Son.Op.101(2)

marcia (It.) march: **alla** —, in march time

marciale (It.) martial, like a march: Medtner Op.14(2)

marinari (It.) sailors: Schum. *Alb.Y.*(36)

markiert (Ger.) marked, emphatic: Schum. Son.Op.22(3) **sehr rasch und** —, very fast and well-marked

marqué (Fr.) marked, stressed: e.g. Albéniz *Iberia* **bien — et "p" cependant**, well marked, but quiet nonetheless

marquées (Fr.) marked (with a sign): Deb. *Images* (1) **toutes les notes — du signe**, all the notes marked with the sign; *PP*(3) **les notes — du signe – expressives et un peu dehors**, the notes marked with the sign – expressive and slightly prominent

marquez (Fr.) stress: Gran. *Goy.*(3) **— le chant à la basse**, stress the tune in the bass; Messiaen *Les Sons Impalpables* **— le chant de la partie intérieure**, stress the tune of the inside part

martelé (Fr.) hammered: Deb. *Études* (3); Gottschalk *Bamboule*; Messiaen *VR*18

martellato (It.) hammered: Bach/Busoni, Barber, Britten, Gottschalk, Gran., Liszt*, Rach., Scho.; Liszt trs. *Norma* — **con strepito**, hammered noisily; *HR* 2, 7, 8 **molto** —, very much hammered

marziale (It.) martial: Grieg Op.56(3) **allegretto** —; Liszt *A de P* 2(3) **andante** —

ma sensa replica (It.) but without repeats: Beeth: Son.Op.10 No.3(3)

mässig (Ger.) moderately, fairly, in moderate time: Hindemith Son.3(3) **— schnell**, fairly fast; Liszt trs. *Lohengrin* — **bewegt**, moving moderately; Scho. Op.23(4) **schwungvoll,** —, full of vigour, in moderate time; Webern Op.27 **sehr** — very moderately

matin d'hiver (Fr.) winter morning: Tch. Op.39

Matrosenlied (Ger.) sailors'-song, sea-shanty: Schum. *Alb.Y.*(37)

mauresque (Fr.) Moorish, of black race

maussade (Ger.) surly, sullen: Satie *Le Prisonnier Maussade*

Mazeppa (Ger.) a heroic Romantic warrior developed by Byron from Voltaire: Liszt, title

mazurka Polish national dance in moderate triple time, with an accent on the second beat. The form spread through Europe in the later eighteenth century and was particularly explored by Chopin (who was Polish): Tch. Op.19(6) **alla** —, in the style of a Mazurka

m.d. (Fr.) **main droit**, the right hand: Deb. *Images* (1) — **en valeur sur le main gauche**, the right hand stronger than the left

meditando (It.) thoughtfully, with contemplation: Clementi Son.Op.50(3); **deliberando e** —

mélancholique (Fr.) melancholy, sad: Gran. *Goy.*(3); Poulenc Noct.(3)

melancolico (It.) melancholy

mêle (Fr.) mingle, mix: Scriabin Son.Op.62

melodia (It.) tune: e.g. Brahms Son.Op.2(2) **sempre ben marcato ed express. la** —, the tune always well marked and expressive: *Hung.Dance* (4) **la** — **forte ed express**, the tune loud and expressive; Grieg Op.63(1) **la** — **sempre mano dextra e molto cantabile**, the tune always with the right hand, and very song-like; Op.62(2) **la** — **molto cantabile**, the tune with a very singing tone

mélodie (Fr.) melody, tune: Scriabin Son.Op.64 **la** — **bien marquée**, the tune well stressed

melodioso (It.) melodious

menaçant (Fr.) menacing: Scriabin Son.Op.64

même (Fr.) same

meno (It.) less; — **mosso** less fast

menthe (Fr.) mint

menuetto (It.) minuet: a moderately fast dance in triple time, often capped with a trio, and placed between the weightier movements of sonatas and symphonies: — **da capo**, go back to the minuet (after the trio)

merle (Fr.) blackbird

mesto (It.) sadly: Barber Son.(3); Bartók *Mikro.*(144); Beeth, Son.Op.10 No.3(2); Brahms Op.117(2); Chopin Maz.Op.33(1); Clementi Son.Op.40(2) **largo, — e patetico**; Liszt *Lugubre Gondola* (2) *HR*2; Scriabin Prél.Op.22(1), 37(1), Maz.Op.25(9)

mesure (Fr.) a musical bar, a rhythmical unit: **en** —, in time; Liszt *A de P*, **pédale à chaque** —, pedal in each bar

mesuré (Fr.) in time (a tempo)

mettez (Fr.) put: Satie *Le piège de Méduse* — **vous dans l'ombre**, put yourself in the background

mezza/o (It.) half: — **voce**, with half the tone: Field Noct.17
   mezzo (for 'mezzoforte')
mf (It.) **mezzoforte**, half loud, quite loud
m.g. (Fr.) **main gauche**, left hand: Deb. *Images*(1) **la main droite
   en valeur sur la** —, the right hand louder than the left
mieux (Fr.) better
mignon(nes) (Fr.) daring, dainty, delicate: Schum. *Carnaval*,
   Alb.Y.(35)
milan noir (Fr.) black kite
minore (It.) minor (key)
minuetto (It.) *see* **menuetto**
misterioso (It.) mysteriously: Brahms Son.Op.5(1); Gran.
   Goy.(6); Liszt *Fanta. on BACH*; Prok. Op.22(1, 2); Rach.
   Op. 42(8); Smetana Op.2(6); Poulenc. Noct.(5) **presto** —;
   Scriabin Son.Op.53(1) — **affanto**, breathlessly mysterious
misticamente (It.) mystically, as in a trance: Busoni *Fanta.
   Contrappuntistica* **piu tranquillo e** —, more peacefully and
   mystically
misura (It.) bar: Britten *Notturne* **senza** —, (without measures),
   in free time
misurato (It.) measured, in strict time: Bach/Busoni *Chaconne*;
   Chopin Noct.Op.15(1); Liszt trs. Overt. *Tannhäuser*
M.M. (Eng., Ger.) **Mälzel's Metronome.** Mälzel developed a
   metronome on a new 'pendulum' principle, but its count of
   'beats per minute' in some older scores is unreliable as a
   guide to speed, and can be taken only as a rough indication.
   (Schumann's metronomic markings are notoriously
   suspect.) Playing to the rigid beat of a metronome has a
   limited use in the early stages of practising a piece but is
   soon abandoned in the interests of more flexible personal
   interpretation, besides being extremely difficult to do.
moderato (It.) in moderate time: next above **allegretto**, next
   below **andantino**: e.g. Fauré *Valse Caprice* Op.62 **molto** —
   quasi lente, very moderate time as if lento; Op.87(22) —
   ma non troppo, in moderate time but not too (much) fast;
   Martinů Son.1 — **poco andante**, a little slower than
   andante
modéré (Fr.) in moderate time, 'moderato': Messiaen *VR4* **ben** —;
   Poulenc Noct.(8) **très** —; *Improvisations* (3) — **mais sans
   lenteur** in moderate time without loitering

modérément (Fr.) moderately: Deb. *Ch.Corner* (1) — **animé**, fairly lively

möglich (Ger.) possible: Schum. Son.Op.22 **so rasch wie** —, as fast as possible; Schollum 7 *Fantasies* (2) **möglichst lebendig**, as lively as possible

moins (Fr.) less

mol (Ger.) minor (key) as contrasted with 'major' (*see* **maggiore**)

molce (It.) soft: Albéniz *Iberia* 'Almérica' **nonchalante e** —, carefree and not rigid

molto (It.) much, very

monotone (Fr.) monotonous, even: Deb. *Epitaph* (6) **doux et** —

montant (Fr.) rising: Satie *Le Fils des Étoiles*

morbidezza (It.) softness, tenderness: Deb. *La Plus que Lente* **con** —, tenderly

morceau (Fr.) morsel, little piece

mordant (Fr.) biting, sharp: Liszt Fanta.Op.2; Poulenc Noct.6 **la note brève et** —, the note short and sharp

morendo (It.) dying away

morendosi (It.) dying away slowly: Gottschalk *Berceuse*

Morgenland (Ger.) the East, land of the rising sun

Morgenwanderer (Ger.) morning-wanderer: Schum. *Alb.Y.*(17)

mormora/endo (It.) muttering, whispering: Busoni *Fanta. on Carmen*, Son'a; Deb. *Études* (2, 4, 7), *Epitaph* (3)

mortuis (L.) *see* **con** — **in lingua mortua**

mosso (It.) moved, with motion: **più** —, faster; **meno** —, less fast

moto (It.) motion: **con** —, quickly

moto perpetuo (It.) perpetual motion – piece consisting of a continued sequence of notes, usually fast, each of the same time value: e.g. Beeth. Son.Op.26(4); Clementi Son.Op.40(1)

mouche (Fr.) fly

mouvement (Fr.) movement, time: **au** —, in time, at the original speed

mouvementé (Fr.) moved, at speed: Satie *Notturno* (3); Deb. *Ch.Corner*; *Images* (1) **un peu au dessous du** —, a little behind the time; *Epitaph* (5) — **de début**, in the original time

m.s. (It.) **mano sinistra**, left hand

muerte (Sp.) death: Gran. *Goy.*(5)

muettes (Fr.) (mutes) soft pedal: Deb. *Nocturne*

munissez vous de clairvoyance (Fr.) provide yourself with clairvoyance: Satie *Gnossienne* (5)

munter (Ger.) lively, brisk: e.g. Schum. *Nov.*Op.2(4), Op.21(8), *Alb.Y.*(2, 10), *Son'a* Op.118(1)

mur (Fr.) wall: Satie, title 'Sur un —', on a wall

murmurando (It.) murmured: Britten Noct.; Liszt trs. Schub. 'Wohin' **dolcissimo** —, very sweetly murmured

murmure (Fr.) murmur: Deb. Prél.(8); Scriabin *Poème* Op.61 **comme un — confus**; like a confused murmur

murmuré (Fr.) murmured, echoed: Scriabin Son.Op.68 **mystérieusement** —

Mutterkin (Ger.) little mother, mummy: Tch. Op.39

muy (Sp.) very

m.v. (It.) **mezza voce**, half-loud

mystèrieusement (Fr.) mysteriously: Messiaen VR1 —, **avec amour**; Scriabin Son.Op.68 — **murmuré**, mysteriously murmured

mystérieux (Fr.) mysterious: Deb. *Estampes* (3); Gran. *Goy*(3); Messiaen VR5 **doux et** —; Poulenc Noct.(1); Ravel *Valses Nobles* (2); Scriabin Prél.Op.67(1) **vague, —**, vague and mysterious

--- N ---

nach (Ger.) after: — **und** —, more and more, little by little, by degrees

Nachklänge (Ger.) recollections, memories: Schum. *Alb.Y.*(25), title

Nacht (Ger.) night; Schum. *Fant.*Op.17

naïf (Fr.) simple: Messiaen VR4 **tendre et** —. tenderly and simply

naissante (Fr.) being born, growing: Scriabin Son.Op.68 **avec une langueur** —, with a dawning listlessness; *Poème* Op.72 **avec une emotion** —, with a growing emotion

naître (Fr.) to be born

n'allez pas plus haut (Fr.) don't go too high: Satie *Danses de Travers*

narrante (It.) narrating, declaiming: Medtner Op.26(7)

nasillard (Fr.) nasal

Nebel (Ger.) mist fog
Nebelgrau (Ger.) grey mist
nel (It.) in the: Mouss. *Pict.*(Promenade)
ne pas se tormenter (Fr.) don't worry, don't torture yourself:
 Satie *Pièces Froides*
ne pas trop manger (Fr.) don't eat too much: Satie *Pièces Froides*
nerveux (Fr.) nervous; Deb. Prél.1(12) — **et avec humour**, lively
 and with humour
ne sortez pas (Fr.) don't leave: Satie *Gnossienne*(20)
nessùn (It.) not any, none
net (Fr.) clear, precise: Deb. *Estampes* (3) — **et vif**, precise and
 lively; *Ch.Corner* (6) **très** — **et très sec**, very precise and
 dry; Poulenc *Novelette* (2) **très** —, very precise;
 Improvisations(9) **très sec et très** —, very dry and precise
nicht (Ger.) not
niedergeschrieben (Ger.) written down
niente (It.) nothing, none, no: Liszt trs. Schub. 'Die Junge
 Nonne' **quasi** —, like nothing (barely audible)
nobilmente (It.) nobly: Liszt trs. *Norma*
noces (Sp.) nights
noch (Ger.) still: — **schneller**, still quickly
nochmals(Ger.) once again: Scho. Op.25 — **anschlagen**, (strike)
 play again
nocturne (Fr.) night piece – a flowing, partly sentimental piece,
 the form originally developed by John Field, used by many
 composers, particularly Chopin, Satie (trs.), Fauré

---- O ----

ottimissimo (It.) optimism: **con** —, optimistically

P

p (It.) **piano** quiet. As many as four **pppp** may be found together.
passacaglia (It.) *see* chaconne
passione (It.) passion: Brahms, Franck, Gottschalk, Liszt*,
   Martinů, Scriabin*, con —, con summa —
pavane (Fr.) ancient slow dance, possibly originating in Padua,
   with a four-beat measured, even processional movement
perdu (Fr.) lost: Satie *Gnossienne* (3)
père (Fr.) father
perlé (Fr.) set with pearls, pearly: Scriabin *Poème* Op.61
   cristallin, —, gem-like, set with pearls
per moto contrario (It.) imitating in contrary motion, the tune
   'upside down': Clementi Son.Op.40(1)
per moto retto (It.) in canon: Clementi Son.Op.40 **Canone I**
   perpetuo —, direct imitation in straight canon
perpetuo (It.) *see* moto —
perpetuum mobile (L.) perpetual motion
pes (It.) *see* pesante
pesamente (It.) heavily, ponderously: Mouss. *Pict.*(2)
pesante (It.) heavily: Albéniz, Bartók, Beeth., Brahms, Britten,
   Chopin, Clementi, Dvořák, Elgar, Gran., Grieg, Liszt,
   Medtner, Mouss., Rach.; Beeth. Son.Op.31(3) **(un) poco**
   —, rather heavily; Liszt *A de P* (2) **sotto voce** —, heavy but
   quiet; Scho. Op.23(5) **molto** —, very heavily; Janáček *Im
   Nebel*; Prok. Son.4(1) **piano ma** —, quiet but weightily
peu (Fr.) a little: — à —, little by little
pezzo (It.) part, movement
Pfade (Ger.) path
Phantasietanz (Ger.) fantastic dance: Schum. *Albumb.*5
phantastisch (Ger.) of fantasy, fantastic: Schum. *Fant.*Op.17
   durchaus — und leidenschaftlich vorzutragen, to be played
   with fantasy and passion throughout
piacere (It.) pleasure. See 'a —'
piacevole (It.) pleasingly, with contentment: e.g. Bartók
   *Mikro.*80; Beeth. Son.Op.31(3), Var.Op.120; Brahms
   Scherzo Op.4; Scriabin *Études* Op.8(4), *Valse* Op.38,
   Morceau Op.45(1); Liszt *Apparitions* (2) — **giocoso**

piangendo (It.) weeping, plaintive: Field Noct.4; Liszt *Lugubre Gondola* (2), *12 Grandes Études* (12)

pianissimo (It.) very quietly

piano (It.) soft, quiet, — **e dolce,** soft and sweet: Beeth. Son.Op.2(1), *see also* 'p'

piccolo (It.) small: Haydn F min.Var. **un — divertimento,** a little amusement

pied (Fr.) foot: à —, on foot

piège (Fr.) trap, snare: Satie, title, 'Le — de Méduse', the snare of Medusa (a Gorgon)

pieghevole (It.) pliable: Medtner Op.11(1)

pie grièche (Fr.) red-backed shrike:Messiaen

pietà (It.) pity, compassion: Gran. *Goy.*(5) **con sentimento de —,** with feeling of pity

pietoso (It.) compassionate, pitying: Liszt *A de P*3 **andante —**

pimpant (Fr.) smart, spruce: Poulenc *Improvisations* (12)

pinçant (Fr.) plucking (string)

pincé (Fr.) (pinched) as if plucked: Deb. *Études* 11

pinson (Fr.) finch

pittoresco (It.) vividly, with colour: Prok. Op.22(7)

più (It.) more: — **mosso,** — **moto,** more moved, faster

pizzicato (It.) as if plucked on a stringed instrument: Schum. Son.Op.11(4) **quasi —;** Brahms Var.Op.21(2), *Pag.Var.* Op.35(2); Poulenc *Improvisations* (9)

placabile (It.) calmly: Medtner Op.11(1)

placido (It.) calm: Liszt *Consolation* (3), *Liebesträume* (1) **lento —** ; *EET*(2) **sempre legato e —;** *A de P*2(6) **lento —**

plainte (Fr.) lament, moan: Deb. *Epitaph* 2 **comme une — loitaine,** like a distant moan

plaintif (Fr.) plaintive: Deb. Prél.1(7) **— e lointain,** plaintive and distant

plaqué (Fr.) (veneered, plated) simultaneous, together, as one

plenissimo (It.) very full: Medtner Op.11(1) **forte —,** the loudest and fullest possible

plénitude (Fr.) fullness: Satie *Choral* No.9

pleno (It.) full: Medtner Op.11(1) **forte —,** maximum volume

plintivo (It.) plaintive: Liszt *HR*2; *A de P*1(8) **recitando —,** plaintive song

pluie (Fr.) rain: Deb. *Estampes* (3) **jardins sous la —,** gardens in the rain; Prok. Op.65(8)

plus (Fr.) more: **de — en —**, more and more

poch(iss)(imo) (It.) very little, the very slightest: Bartók, Chopin, Prok., Schum., Scriabin; Strav. Son.(1924) — **rit**, a very light slowing down; Medtner Op.65(1) — **rit**; Op.11(1) — **calando**, very slightly fading away

pochetino (It.) a tiny bit, a mite: Deb. *Études* 9 — **rubato** very slightly rubato, *cf* Tch. Op.37a(3); — **meno**, a very little less

poco (It.) a little, 'rather' — **a —**, little by little, gradually; — **meno mosso**, a little less movement; Liszt *A de P* 3(1) **un — piu marcato (ma —)**, with a little more stress (but only a little)

poetico (It.) poetical: Scriabin Prél.Op.48(2) — **con delizio**, radiantly poetical

poi (It.) then: — **a —**, little by little

poissons d'or (Fr.) goldfish

Polacca (It.) Polonaise: Chopin Pol.Op.44 **Tempo di —; alla —**, in the style of a Polonaise

Polka (Czech) quick Bohemian dance in 3/4 time: Tch.Op.39

Polonaise Polish national dance form or procession, freely adopted by many nineteenth-century composers, but developed expressively by Chopin with a great variety of tone and mood. It is usually in triple time, with a strong beat followed by paired semi-quavers. There is a basic 'sandwich' form – which Chopin develops freely in the intricacies of his great *Polonaise-Fantasie* Op.61

polymodalité (Fr.) Messiaen in *VR5* employs three of his distinctive modes or scales at the same time, one on each stave. (These modes differ from earlier ecclesiastical modes, and were developed for his own use.)

Pomp (Ger.) ceremonial, pomp, swagger: Schum. Hum.Op.20 **mit einigem —**

pomposo (It.) pompously, with ceremony: Deb. *Études* (11), Schum. Son.Op.11(3); Liszt *Mephisto Waltz* 3; Pol.(2) **allegro — con brio**; Saint-Saëns *Carnival* **allegretto —**

ponctué (Fr.) punctuated: Poulenc *Improvisations* (12)

pont (Fr.) bridge: Satie, title, 'Sur Le —'

portamento (It.) carrying on, half-staccato: Medtner Op.1(8)

portez cela plus loin (Fr.) take this further: Satie *Gnossienne* (3)

posato (It.) emphasised: Busoni *Fanta. Contrappuntistica* possible (Fr., It.) possible: Liszt Fanta.Op.2, *2 Concert Studies* (2), *HR*2 **il piu presto** —, as fast as possible; Schum. Op.14(1) **prestissimo** —; *Ét.Symp.* (9) **presto** —

postulez en vous-même (Fr.) question yourself: Satie *Gnossienne* (1)

pouce (Fr.) thumb

poupée (Fr.) doll: Tch. Op.39

Präludium (Ger.) prelude

précédent (Fr.) preceding: Deb. *Images.* (2) **au movement** —, at the preceding speed

precedente (It.) preceding, previous: Rach. Son.Op.28 **tempo** —, in the previous time

précieusement (Fr.) preciously, affectedly

precipitando (It.) precipitately, headlong: Janáček *Im Nebel*; Lut. *Alb.Y.*(8); Prok. Op.84(3); Scriabin Prél.Op.48(4)

precipitatissimo (It.) headlong, very precipitate: Scriabin Prél. Op.48(1)

precipitato (It.) headlong, plunging: Liszt*; Prok. Son.Op.83(3); Franck Ball.Op.9

preciso (It.) precisely, exactly: Schum. *Ét.Symp.*Op.13(Finale)

prelude (Fr.) in origin, a shortish preliminary to a larger and more serious work, but later developed as a short, often introspective, piece in its own right (or perhaps as a prelude to 'heightened awareness'), notably by Chopin, Deb. and Rach.

premier mouvement (Fr.) in the original time: Deb. *Études* (5); Messiaen *VR*6 (*see also* **1er**)

prenez (Fr.) take: Satie *Le piège de Méduse*

près (Fr.) borders, environs: Prok. Op.65(12)

près (Fr.) near: Deb. *Études* (10)

presque (Fr.) nearly, almost: Poulenc Imp.(3) — **sans pédale**, almost without pedal

pressant (Fr.) hurrying: Albéniz *Iberia* en — **peu à peu**, hurrying little by little

presser (Fr.) to hurry: **sans** —, without haste

prestezza (It.) speed: Liszt *EETF*

prestissimo (It.) very fast (next below **presto**)

presto (It.) fast: — **possible**, as fast as possible: Rach. Prél.32(4); Poulenc *Improvisations* (9); Liszt *A de P*1(5) — **furioso**; Liszt *Robert le Diable* **il piu** — **possible**. (Next above

prestissimo, next below **allegrissimo**)
prière du matin (Fr.) morning prayer: Tch.Op.39
primo (It.) first: **con** —, as at first
principio (It.) beginning: Sch. *Dances of the Dolls* (4) **tempo del**

profond (Fr.) deep: Deb. *Études* (10) **expressif et** —
profondément (Fr.) deeply: Satie *Prél. de la Porte* — **doux**
promèner, se promèner (Fr.) walk, move, cover ground: Prok.
  Op.65(12)
prononcé (Fr.) pronounced, articulated: Messiaen *F d J* **bien** —,
  clair et mélodique
pronunziato (It.) pronounced, stated: Liszt trs. Schub. 'Auf dem
  Wasser' **ben — il canto**, sound the tune clearly: *12 Grandes
  Études* (6), *EETF*(6) **ben — ed expressivo il canto;**
  Apparitions **molto — la melodia**
propice (Fr.) propitious, with good weather: Deb. *Epitaph* 2
  pour que la nuit soit —
propre (Fr.) one's own, of oneself
puerto (Sp.) port, harbour
pugno (It.) fist, *see* **col** —
puissant (Fr.) powerful: Scriabin Son.Op.70
punktierte (Ger.) dotted (notes)
pur (Fr.) pure: Scriabin Son.Op.64 —, **limpide**, pure, clear;
  Son.Op.70 **très doux et** —, very sweet and pure

—— **Q** ——

quarto (It.) group of four notes (e.g. in a crotchet, or like a
  triplet)
quasi (It.) like, as, almost: Beeth. Bag.Op.126(5) — **allegretto;** —
  violoncello, like a cello: Liszt trs. Schub. 'Ständchen'
quejas (Sp.) complaints, laments
Quelle (Ger.) spring, source
quietissimo (It.) as quietly as possible: Scriabin Son.Op.30(1)
quieto (It.) quiet, calm: Beeth. Son.Op.78(1); Liszt *12 Grandes
  Études* (5) — **expressivo**; Fanta.Op.2 **dolce — teneramente,**

sweetly, quietly, and tenderly

quodlibet (L.) as you like, what pleases: J.S. Bach, *Goldberg Variations* (30). An ingenious intermingling of popular tunes

---

——R——

Raben (Ger.) raven
raddolcente (It.) softening: Liszt *PE6*
radieux (Fr.) radiant: Scriabin Son.Op.70
rad(d)olcendo (It.) becoming sweeter, gentler, again: Liszt *12 Grandes Études* (6, 9); *EET*(9); Chopin *Allegro* Op.46
rafrâichire (Fr.) refresh: Satie *Le piège de Méduse*
rageur (Fr.) violent, in a rage: Deb. Prél.1(9)
raideur (Fr.) stiffness: Deb. *Epitaph 5*
ralenti(r) (Fr.) slow down (*see* **rallentando**), held back: Poulenc *Novelette* **absolument sans** —, absolutely without slowing down; Ravel *Gaspard* **sans** —
ralentissant (Fr.) slowing down: Satie *Petit Prélude*; Ravel *Menuet Antique*
rall(entando) (It.) slowing down, slackening
rallentare (It.) to slow down
rapide (Fr.) rapid, fast
rappel (Fr.) recall
rapprochant (Fr.) drawing in: Deb. Prél.2(12)
rasch (Ger.) quick, fast: Berg Son.Op.1; Schum. Son.Op.22 **so —
wie möglich ... schneller**, as fast as possible ... faster
rattenendo (It.) gradually holding back: Scriabin Son.Op.30(2)
rauschend (Ger.) noisy: Schum. *Nov*.Op.21(4) — **und festlich**
ravissement (Fr.) rapture: Scriabin Son.Op.70 **avec — et tendresse**, ravishing and tenderly
Rechte (Ger.) right hand
récit (Fr.) recitative: Ravel; *Miroirs* 4, **en récit/recitativo**, like a recitative or free-style solo voice
recitando (It.) reciting, like speech, like a recitative in a sung work: Liszt trs. Schub. 'Der Wanderer'; *Lugubre Gondola* (2);

Grieg Ball.Op.24 — **stretto**, drawing in the threads of song
recitativ(o) (It.) with free-flowing song, like a recitative: Beeth.
Son.Op.110(3); Busoni *Fanta. Contrappuntistica* — **drammatica ma sempre continuando**, as a dramatic recitative but always keeping to the time; Chopin Noct.Op.32(1); Liszt*; Gran. *Danses* (11), *Esc.Rom.*(1, 5) **recitativisch ad lib**, freely as a recitative
reflet (Fr.) reflection
refrapper (Fr.) to strike again: Deb. *Études* (7) **reprendre avec la main droit sans —**, repeat with the right hand without restriking the tied notes
reich (Ger.) rich: Mouss. *Pict.*(6)
Reihe (Ger.) series, row
Reiselied (Ger.) (journey-song) recessional: Grieg Op.17(13)
Reiter (Ger.) rider: Schum. *Alb.Y.*(23) **Reiterstück**, tune for a horseman
relâche (Fr.) relaxation, rest: Satie *Entr'acte Symphonique*
religioso (It.) religiously, churchily: Liszt trs. Schub. 'Die Junge Nonne'
remercier la pluie au matin (Fr.) giving thanks for morning rain: Deb. *Epitaph* 6
remise (Fr.) remission, forgiveness: Satie *Danses Gothiques*
repentirs (Fr.) remorse; Prok. Op.(5)
repetizione (It.) repetition: Beeth: Son.Op.26(2) **la prime parte senza —**, the first part without repetition
replica (It.) repeat
reprendre (Fr.) take up again, repeat: Deb. *PP*(1) **— le mouvement**, recover speed; Messiaen *Le Nombre Léger* **— peu à peu le 1er.mvt.**, return gradually to the original speed
reprenez (Fr.) take up again, repeat: **— la mouvement**, revert to the original time
requiebros (Sp.) compliments (amorous), flirtatious remarks: Gran. *Goy.*(2)
respirer (Fr.) breathe, have respite, relent: Poulenc, *Improvisation* (6) **sans —, strictement en mesure**
retard(er) (Fr.) hold back: Satie *Désespoir*; Deb. *PP*(1)
retenant (Fr.) holding back, slowing down: Deb. Prél.1(4), 1(8), 2(3); Satie *Entr'acte Symphonique*
retenez (Fr.) hold back
retenu (Fr.) held back, slowed down

rêvant (Fr.) dreaming: Scriabin Op.71(2)

rêve (Fr.) dream: Scriabin *Poème* Op.61 **comme en une —**, as in a dream; Op.62 **le — prends forme**, the dream takes shape

rêveur (Fr.) dreamy: Deb. *Prél.*2(4) **doux et —**; Albéniz *Iberia*

rêveusement (Fr.) dreamily: Satie *Le Poisson Rêveur*

rêvez doucement (Fr.) dream sweetly: Satie *Deux Rêveries*

rhythmé (Fr.) [1] rhythm/movement in either sense: Deb. Prél.1(6) **ce — doit avoir la valeur sonore d'un fond de paysage triste et glacé**, the tonal quality of a country valley sad and frozen; **très —**, with marked rhythm; Deb. *PP*1; Poulenc *Suite* (2), *Novellettes* (2); Gottschalk *Sambouca* **Bon —**; Albéniz Op.47(4) [2]

ricordanza (It.) memorial: Gran. *Goy.*(5) **malinconico —**, sad memorial

rideau (Fr.) curtain (of a theatre): Satie *Prélude de la Porte*

ridicolo (It.) ridiculous: Saint-Saëns *Carnival* (12)

ridiculosamente (It.) ridiculously, mockingly: Prok. Op.22(10)

rien (Fr.) nothing: Deb. *Images* (2) **presque —**, images reduced to 'almost nothing'

rifendendo (It.) recapturing

Rigaudon (Fr., Eng.) lively Provençal dance in duple or quadruple time

Riggadon *see* **Rigaudon**

rigore (It.) strictness, inflexibility, *see* **senza**

rigoureux (Fr.) rigorous, strict: Deb. *Estampes* (3) **1ère temps, moins —**, in the first time, but less strictly

rinforzando, rinforzato (It.) reinforcing: Beeth.*, Chopin, Clementi, Deb., Haydn, Liszt*, Schub., Schum.

riprendendo (It.) repeating, taking up again: Barber *Waltz* Op.29 **— il tempo**, recovering the time

riso ironico (It.) with an ironic laugh: Scriabin *Poèmes* Op.36

risoluto (It.) fast and with drive: Albéniz, Bartók, Beeth., Brahms, Busoni, Chopin, Clementi, Deb., Franck, Gran., Grieg, Kuhlau, Medtner, Rach.

rit(artando) (It.) holding back, slowing: Scho. Op.25 *Gigue* **Ohne —**, without slowing down

ritardare (It.) to slow: Medtner, Op.55(1) **largamento, lugubrae, ma non —**, becoming broader and gloomier, but not slowing down

ritendendo (It.) holding back: Beeth. Son.Op.110, 111,

Var.Op.120

ritenuto (It.) (retain) slow down

ritmato (It.) with marked rhythm, stressed: Bartók *Mikro* 112, 116

ritmico (It.) rhythmically: Gran. *Goy*(1) **a tempo e —**, in strict time and rhythm; *Goy*.6, **— staccato**; Ireland *Son'a* (3); Poulenc *Improvisations* (1) **presto —**

ritornello (It.) a fragment of music (descended from a refrain) which returns at intervals and so denotes sections of a larger movement; Liszt Schub. trs. 'Die Junge Nonne', 'Gretchen', 'Der Lindenbaum'

ritournelle/o (It.) 'return' as in a round: Satie *Gambades*

Ritterliches Tor (Ger.) the 'Gates' of the knights, the 'Golden Gate' of Kiev: Mouss. *Pict*(10)

Ritter von Steckenpferd (Ger.) Schum. *Ksz.*(9), title, knight on a hobby-horse

robusto (It.) robust, sturdy: Bartók *Mikro*.92 **allegro —**

rondeau (Fr.) **rondo** (It.) a piece based on recurring and revolving themes. Rondos were written in many moods (though lightness predominates), and either as entities or as concluding parts of suites and sonatas. Their outstanding characteristic is the return round (rondo) to a repeated tune (which may be varied)

rondenas (Sp.) Spanish dance for two

rondoletto (It.) a small rondo: Schum. Son.Op.118(1)

rossignol (Fr.) nightingale

rouge-gorge (Fr.) robin

roulement (Fr.) rumbling of drums (Messiaen)

rousserole turdoïde (Fr.) great reedwarbler: Messiaen *FdJ*

rovescio (It.) reverse, *see* **al —**

rubato (It.) by this romantic approach time is 'robbed' (being kept to order by the accompaniment) and repaid at the climactic moment (of a phrase or much longer passage), so that there is some tension between tune and accompaniment, which continues to uphold the bar structure: Deb. *La Plus Que Lente Valse* **molto — con morbidezza**, very rubato and tenderly; Sho. Son.2.Op.61(1), **largo molto —**

Rückblick (Ger.) backward glance, retrospect: Brahms Son.Op.5(4)

rude (Fr.) rough, uncouth: Poulenc *Improvisations* (6); Satie

Choral No.7

rudement (Fr.) roughly

Ruh (Ger.) peace, quiet: Schum. Op.4(2) Liszt trs. Schub. 'Du bist die Ruh'

ruhig (Ger.) quiet, still: Liszt trs. *Lohengrin* — **bewegt**: gently moving; Hindemith Son.1 *Die Lorelei* **sehr — und gebunden**

Rundgesang (Ger.) a (sung) round: Schum. *Alb.Y.*(22)

Russico (It.) Russian: **nel modo —**, in the Russian manner

———— **S** ————

sagement (Fr.) quietly: Deb. *Études* (1)

salut (Fr.) well-being, health: Satie, title, **'Prière pour le — de mon âme'**

samt (Ger.) together with: Schub., title, **Marsch — Trio**

sanft (Ger.) gentle, easy, soft: Beeth. Op.110 **con amabilita, —**, with tender affection; Brahms Op.76(6) **— bewegt**, moving gently; Mn Op.7(1) **— und mit Empfindung**, gently and with feeling

sans sourciller (Fr.) without frowning, without turning a hair: Satie *Pièces Froides* 2

sans top frémir (Fr.) without trembling too much: Satie *Le Fils Des Étoiles*

s'apaisant (Fr.) *see* **apaisant**

sarabande (Fr., It., Ger.) ancient, slow and noble dance in triple time but with a tendency to the rhythm of minim, semibreve: Deb. *Images* (1) **dans le style d'une — mais sans rigeur**

sauterelles (Fr.) grasshoppers: Prok. Op.59(2)

sauvage (Fr.) savage: Scriabin Prél.Op.59(2)

savamment (Fr.) knowingly: Satie *Gnossienne* (6), *Petite Ouvert.*

scandé (Fr.) chanted, well marked: Satie *Petite Ouvert.* **le chant bien en dehors et très —**, the song well to the fore and well marked

Scarbo a clown's name from Ravel *Gaspard* (3)

schalkhaft (Ger.) roguish, as a joke: Schum. *Alb.Y.*(11)

Schalmeienklang (Ger.) sound of (shawms) pipes

scherz(ando) (It.) as a joke, playfully: Barber, Bartók, Beeth., Brahms, Chopin, Deb., Elgar, Field, Grieg, Hindemith, Kuhlau, Liszt, Medtner, Mn, Mouss., Scho., Schub., Schum., Scriabin, Smetana, Strav.

scherzare (It.) to joke: Deb. *Études* 3, 11

scherzino (It.) little joke

scherzo (It.) a joke; typically a lighter movement after or before pieces of greater intensity, but developed in the nineteenth century as a generally brisk triple time piece on its own: Beeth. Son.Op.28; Brahms *Scherzo* Op.4; Mn *Scherzo B min.*; Mouss. *Pict.*5; Schum. *Fasch.*

scherzoso (It.) roguishly, as a joke: Liszt *Mephisto Waltz* 3; Schum. *Alb.Y.*(11); Scriabin Prél.Op.35(3)

schlägt (Ger.) strikes: Schum. *Pap.*Op.2

schleppen (Ger.) drag, hold back: Berg. Son.Op.1 **nicht** —

Schleppend (Ger.) dragging, drawing back: Beeth. Var.Op.120; Bach/Busoni *Chaconne* **feierlich gemessen, doch nicht** —

Schloss (Ger.) castle: Mouss. *Pict.*

Schlummerlied (Ger.) slumber-song, lullaby: Schum. *Albumb.*(16)

Schluss (Ger.) end, conclusion

Schmetterling (Ger.) butterfly

Schnitterliedchen (Ger.) little harvest song: Schum. *Alb.Y.*(18)

Schottische (Ger.) nineteenth-century Scottish dance in duple time

schwächer (Ger.) softer, weaker

schwebend (Ger.) suspended, undecided, wavering: Scho. Op.105(2)

Schwermut (Ger.) melancholy, depression

scintillante(e) (Fr.) scintillating, sparkling: Deb. Prél.2(8)

sciolto (It.) nimbly, with agility: Brahms, Handel Var.Op.24(14); Liszt *Apparitions* (2)

scorrevole (It.) flowing, sliding: Bartók *Mikro.*(85)

sec(co), sèche (It., Fr.) dry, crisp, without much tone: Albéniz *Iberia* **rudement marqué,** — **et précis**; Barber Op.28 **staccato e** —, **senza ped.**; Bartók *Mikro*124 — **quasi pizzo,** as dry as if plucked; Deb. *Ch.Corner* **très net et très** —; Liszt *Mephisto Waltz* 3; Poulenc *Improvisation 1* **harmonie très**

—, the harmony very precise; Noct.5 — et très rhythmé; *Improvisations* presto très —

sécheresse (Fr.) dryness: Satie *Sonneries de la Rose* détaché sans —, detached without dryness

s'effacent (Fr.) *see* effacent

se fixer (Fr.) settle down: Satie *Piéces Froides*

segno (It.) the sign indicating the start of new material or material to be repeated (𝄋)

seguenti (It.) following

seguidillas (Sp.) a dance in triple time: Albéniz Op.47(7)

Sehnsucht (Ger.) yearning, romantic longing

sehnsüchtig (Ger.) with longing: Mn Op.7(6); Liszt trs. Chopin 'Löse Himmel'

sehnsuchtsvoll (Ger.) filled with longing: Beeth. Son.Op.101(3)

sehr (Ger.) very

seliger Tod (Ger.) happy/blessed death: Liszt *Liebestraume* 2

s'eloignant (Fr.) *see* eloignant

semplice (It.) simply

semplicita (It.) simplicity: Gran. *Esc.Rom.*(2) con molta —; Prok. Op.22(1) con una — espressiva

sempre (It.) always: — di più, ever more and more

sensibile (It.) sensitive: Deb. *Études* 4 dolce —

sentier (Fr.) path

sentimentale (Fr.) sentimental, with feeling: Tch. Op.19(4) andante —

sentimento (It.) feeling: con intimo —, with intimate feeling, Beeth., Brahms, Chopin, Gran., Liszt*, Schum.*; Brahms Ball.Op.10(4) con intimissimo —, Schum. Hum.Op.20 innig (con —); *Kreis.*(2) con profundo —; Liszt Son.(2) B min. dolcissimo —

senza (It.) without: — replica, without repeat, — repetizio, without repeat, — ornamenti, without ornaments; Clementi Son.Op.12; Chopin Noct.Op.9(3), 15(2) — rigore, without strictness, flexibly; Chopin Noct.Op.9 — tempo, outside the counted beat; Schum. *Allegro* Op.8

se raccorder (Fr.) join up, link up: Satie *Danses de Travers* (2)

serenata (Sp.) serenade

serioso (It.) seriously: Beeth. Var.Op.120 allegro ma non troppo e —; Grieg Op.57(3) allegretto —; Prok. Son.4(2)

serrant (Fr.) pressing on, accelerating: Deb. Prél.1(7) en — et

augmentant beaucoup, pressing forward and broadening:
Deb. *Epitaph* 3 en — un peu; Deb. *Images* (2) en — jusqu'à
la fin, accelerating towards the end; Deb. *La Plus Que
Lente Valse* rubato ... en — ... rubato ... en —

serré(s) (Fr.) close, tight, squeezed: Ravel *Miroirs* (4) les arpéges
très —, the arpeggios very close together; Poulenc
Promenade (1939)

serrez (Fr.) press on, accelerate

s'éteignant (Fr.) *see* éteignant

seul (Fr.) alone

sfogato (It.) given vent, expressed, light easy: Chopin *Barcarolle*
Op.60 dolce —; Liszt *HR*14 — con bravura

sf., sforzando, sforzato (It.) strongly accented, suddenly loud

Siciliano Sicilian dance in 6/8 time and sad mood: Schum.
Alb.Y.(11)

siebenbürgisch (Ger.) Transylvanian, Romano-Hungarian

silencieusement (Fr.) silently: Satie *Le piège de Méduse*

silenza (It) silence

simile/i (It.) similarly

simplice (It.) simple

simplicité (Fr.) simplicity: Satie *Reverie du Pauvre* avec un humble
et douce —

sin(o) (It.) until: — al fine, until the end; Field Noct.16

singbar (Ger.) like a song, cantabile: Beeth. Son.Op.90(2) nicht
zu geschwind un sehr — vorzutragen, not too fast and with
a very singing tone

singe (Fr.) monkey; Satie *Le piège de Méduse* (2)

singend (Ger.) singing, cantabile: Schum. *Davidsbündler* (14)
zart und —, tender and singing

sinistra (It.) left (hand): Grieg Op.66(8) ben marcato mano —,
the left hand well marked

slargando (It.) slowing, broadening: Liszt *Consolation* (4); *HR*4;
Franck *Prél., Aria, Finale*; Gran. *Dansas* 9

slentando, slentare (It.) slowing: Chopin Pol.Op.40(2);
Prél.Op.28(15); Ball.Op.38; Clementi Son.Op.12(2);
Ireland Son.(1); Medtner Op.26(4); Liszt Son.Bmin.(3),
HPR(9), *A de P*1(9); *3 Concert Studies* (1); *Apparitions* (2)
Liszt *Soir.*(4), *A de P*2(5) senza —

smorzando (It.) extinguishing, dying down: Bartók, Beeth.,
Brahms, Chopin, Clementi, Deb., Dussek, Field, Kuhlau,

Liszt, Schub. Schum., Scriabin

soave (It.) gentle: Brahms Handel Var.Op.24(12); Liszt *Gretchen*; Scriabin *Poème* Op.61; Gran. *Danses* (11)

soft pedal the left-hand of the two (or three) piano pedals has a different mechanism and effect in the upright from that in the grand piano. In the upright, the pedal levers bring all the hammer heads closer to their strings so that hammer-travel and tonal output are reduced. In the grand (**una corda**) mechanism, the keyboard and action slide sideways so that a reduced number of the normal number of strings for each note is struck. This produces a distinct change in tone as well as in volume. There have been other short-lived devices for mechanical reduction, often being by interposing a strip of felt or other material between hammers and strings (sometimes known as the **céleste** method). Any of these arrangements may be indicated by **una corda** or **u.c.** in the score

sognando (It.) dreaming: Medtner Op.11(1); Prok. Op.84(2) **andante** —

soigneusement (Fr.) carefully: Satie *Exercices*

soir (Fr.) evening

solamente (It.) only

solenne (It.) solemn, religious: Liszt trs. *Parsifal*

solennel (Fr.) solemn, grave: Messiaen *VR5* **lumineux et** —; *VR18* — **mais un peu vif**; *VR20* **très lent,** —

sombre (Fr.) dark, sombre: Ravel *Miroirs* (2) — **et lointain**; Albéniz *Iberia* — **et sonore**; Poulenc *Impromptu 5*

somma (It.) utmost; Liszt **con** — **passione** e.g. *A de P*1(9)

sommessamente (It.) soft, low: Busoni *Fanta. Contrappuntistica*

songerie (Fr.) dreaming, reverie

sonata (It.) ('sounded' on instrument(s) as distinct from the voice). A piece for one or two instruments which evolved in fairly strict form from collections of varied Suites, and whose purpose was partly display. Any part or 'movement' of a Sonata, but particularly the first, might follow the gradually accustomed 'Sonata Form', exploring a limited number of subjects in related musical keys and consisting broadly of Exposition, Development and Recapitulation, often ending with a brilliant Coda. Then there tended to follow a slow movement (often variations of some solem-

nity), and either a Minuet with Trio, or a Scherzo as relief
before a weightier final fast movement, which might be of
Rondo form or again in Sonata Form. Thus the typical classical Sonata was a sandwich of four or five subtly related
'movements'. The mature Beethoven wrote Sonatas to
other designs, often with 'flashbacks' to earlier material,
and in only two or in linked movements. Liszt's towering
Sonata in B Minor is nominally all in a single movement.
Whatever the actual structure, the word Sonata became
synonymous with exploration of material and display of
serious musical intelligence (as well as technical performing
skill) in an instrumental (predominantly solo) piece, over a
period of some 200 years.

Sonnabendnacht (Ger.) Saturday night

sonoramente (It.) sonorously: Prok. Son.5(1)

sonoré (Fr.) sonorous, of full sound: Deb. *Images* 2(1) **doucement** —; Scriabin Son.Op.64 **mystérieusement** —; Albéniz
Iberia 'El Puerto' **aussi — que possible**; Strav. Son.(2) **un
poco piu** —

sonorité (Fr.) sound, tone: Deb. *Estampes* **dans une — plus
claire**, with a brighter tone; Ravel *Pavane* **assez doux, mais
d'une — large**, quite gentle but with a full sound; Messiaen
Prél., *La Colombe* **d'une — très enveloppée**, with a soft and
distant sound

sonoro (It.) **sonore** (Fr.) sonorous, with full tone: Albéniz
Op.47(4), (13)

soppresso (It.) suppressed: Busoni *Fanta. Contrappuntistica*
molto expressivo, ma con un sentimento —, very expressively yet with sentiment suppressed

sopra (It.) above, over, before, 1) one part louder than another;
2) one hand passing over the other: 3) **come** —, as above,
as before

sorcière (Fr.) sorceress, witch: Tch. Op.39(19)

sordamento (It.) muffled: Medtner Op.11(1)

sordinai/o (It.) mute, damper: **Con** — may mean 'with the
dampers on' (i.e. without the sustaining pedal) or 'with the
soft pedal'. a) Beeth. Son.Op.27 No.2(1), **senza** —, without
dampers, i.e. with sustaining pedal; b) Debussy *Études* 4;
con —; c) Schub. Son.Op.143(2) may use the soft pedal.
The dampers/mutes can be applied (as required by **con** —)

by using the left-hand 'soft' pedal, but the softening here is not produced by 'mutes', rather by string reduction. The effect depends on the design of the piano; only in an upright piano is a further 'mute' added, and then not to the strings but by limiting the hammers' movement. *See* céleste

sospirando (It.) sighing, yearning

sostenendo (It.) sustaining: Busoni *Son'a ad Usum Infantis* (3)

sostenutissimo (It.) intensely, sustained: Busoni *Fanta. Contrappuntistica*

sosten(uto) (It.) sustained: Deb. *Études* 5 — **e marcato**; Clementi Son.Op.39(3) **largo pathetico e** —; Chopin Fanta.Op.49 **lento** —; Prok. Op.22(9) — **e dolce**; Grieg *Ballade* Op.24 — **e furioso**

sostenuto pedale (Eng., It.) a third (middle) pedal is increasingly being fitted to American and Continental pianos. It enables selective retention of lower notes by holding their dampers up, whilst most of the piano remains damped

sotto (It.) under, beneath: a) one part quieter than another; b) one hand passing under the other; c) — **voce**, very quietly; Schum. *Ét.Symph.*Op.13(11) — **voce ma marcato**; Liszt *Soir.*(1) — **voce, marcato expressivo**; Liszt *A de P*2 — **voce pesante**; Liszt trs. *Trovatore* — **voce marcato e pesante**

souffle (Fr.) breath: Scriabin Son.Op.62, — **mysterieux**

souple (Fr.) supple: Deb. *Epitaph* 4 — **et sans rigueur**; Ravel *Miroirs* **D'un rhythme** —; Messiaen VR19 — **et suave**; Albéniz *Iberia* —, **très doux et lointain**, **pppp**, liquid, very sweet and distant, extremely quiet

sourd (Fr.) (deaf) dull, hollow, muffled: Deb. Prél.1.10; Deb. *Masques* — **et en s'eloignant**; Messiaen VR16 — **et lointain**

sourdement (Fr.) dully, muffled: Deb. *Études* 5 — **tumultueux**, with muffled violence

sourdine (Fr.) mute, soft pedal (*see* **sordino**): Ravel *Gaspard* — **durant toute la pièce**, soft pedal throughout; Deb. *Études* 5 **gardez la** —, keep the soft pedal on and vary the sustaining pedal; Ravel *Gaspard* (3) — **mais f**, with soft pedal but played loud

soutenu (Fr.) **sostenuto** (It.) sustained: Deb. *Hommage à Haydn* **doux et soutenu**

Spass (Ger.) fun, merriment

spianoto (It.) smoothed, running on evenly: Chopin Op.22

andante —; Gran. *Esc.Rom.* 6 andantino —

spiccato (It.) articulated, staccato: Busoni *Fanta. on Carmen*

Spiegelbild (Ger.) mirror image, reflection

Spiel (Ger.) game

spielen (Ger.) to play: Tch. Op.39

spirito (It.) spirit: Beeth., Chopin, Clementi*, Dussek, Liszt, con —, spirited

spiritoso (It.) with spirit

spirituel (Fr.) spiritual: Deb. Prél.2 — et discrèt, inward and withdrawn

sposso (It.) exhausted, worn out: Schum. Op.23 — ritenere, hold back exhausted

spozalizio (It.) wedding

Springar Norwegian dance in triple time

staccatissimo (It.) extremely short, highly 'staccato': Brahms Son.Op.1(2); Liszt *Czardas Macabre*; Bach/Busoni *Chaconne*; Liszt *Rhapsody Espagnole*; Franck Op.5

staccato (It.) removed, 'shortened'. Although some composers specify types of staccato, the small variety available is usually dictated by the particular piano action, and expressions such as the following point more to spirit than to an achievable effect: Prok. Son.Op.84 molto —; Schu. Op.23, Op.33 — scherzando; Liszt *Almira* — e distintamente; Liszt *Robert le Diable*

stärker (Ger.) stronger, louder, fuller tone

steigender (Ger.) increasing: Mn Op.7 mit — Lebhaftigkeit, with increasing vigour

stesso (=istesso) (It.) same

stets (Ger.) still, yet, always, ever

Stimme (Ger.) voice, part: Schum. Hum. Op.20 innere —, a hidden internal part; *Nov.*Op.21(7) — aus der Ferne, voice from afar

Stimmungsbilder (Ger.) 'sound-pictures': Medtner Op.1.; R. Strauss Op.9

straff (Ger.) strict: Schum. *Alb.Y.*(2)

strappato (It.) torn, ripped: Busoni *Fanta. on Carmen*

stravaganza (It.) extravagance, eccentricity: Scriabin Son.Op.53; Prél.Op.31(3) con — extravagantly

streg im Takt (Ger.) strictly in time;: Liszt *12 Grandes Études* (2, 8)

Streit (Ger.) strife, squabble: Mouss. *Picts.* — der Kinder nach

dem Spiel, children's quarrels after playing

strepito, strepitoso (It.) noisily: *see* **con —**; Deb. *Études* 1, 5; Liszt *12 Grandes Études* (4) **con — sempre fff;** Prok. Son.Op.103(2); Liszt Fanta.Op.2 **— marcatissimo**

strette (Fr.) drawing together, *see* **stretto**

stretto (It.) drawing together, pressing on; e.g. Grieg Op.47(1) **— molto e crescendo;** Sibelius Op.34 **poco a poco più —,** more and more drawing together

strident (Fr.) shrill: Deb. Prél.1(7), 11(12)

string(endo) (It.) speeding up, pressing on: Barber, Bartók, Berg, Britten, Brahms, Chopin, Deb., Dvořák, Elgar, Grieg, Liszt, R. Strauss, Tch.; Beeth. Bag.Op.119(6); Schum. *Carnaval* **— semper piu e piu,** press on more and more; Liszt *12 Grandes Études* (1) **— ma semper largamente,** drawing in but without loss of breadth

stringere (It.) 'squeeze', increase speed gradually: Deb. *Études* 4

Stück (Ger.) (piece) movement, section

Stückchen (Ger.) little piece: Schum. *Alb.Y.*(5)

Stücklein (Ger.) little piece: Schum. *Drei Stücklein*

suave (Fr., Sp.) smooth, even: Messiaen VR19, **souple et —,** supple and even

sub(ite) (Fr.) sudden

subito (It.) at once, immediately

sucer (Fr.) to suck: Satie *Pièces Froides* (2)

sulla morte d'un Éroe (Fr.) on the death of a hero: Beeth. Son.Op.26(3)

suono (It.) sound: Fauré Op.17(3) **con — sonorously**

supérieur (Fr.) upper: Ravel *Valses Nobles* (8) **la partie — en dehors,** the upper part standing out

suppliant (Fr.) imploring: Deb. Prél.1(9)

supra (It.) on, above

surgit (Fr.) surges, rises into view: Scriabin Son.Op.62

sur la langue (Fr.) on the (tip of the) tongue: Satie *Gnossienne* 1

surren (Ger.) hum, buzz

surtout (Fr.) especially, particularly

suspirante (Sp.) sighing: Gran. *Esc.Rom*(5)

sustaining pedal the true name of the right-hand pedal (often mis-called 'loud pedal'). Depressing the pedal causes all the dampers to rise, leaving the vibrations of all their strings' harmonics to intermingle

T

Takt (Ger.) beat, time, tempo: **streng in —**, in strict time
tambour(o) (Fr.) drum: Deb. Prél.1(12) **quasi —**, like a drum
tango Argentinian dance
tanto (It.) too much: **non —**, not too much
Tanz, Tänzer (Ger.) dance(s)
Tanzlied (Ger.) dancing song: Tch. Op.39(xvii)
Tarantella (It.) very lively Italian dance in 6/8 time, supposed to
    have originated as an exorcism for the bite of the tarantula
    spider, e.g. Chopin, Liszt
tardo (It.) slow: Schub. Son. E.maj. **più —**, more slowly
Tasten (Ger.) keys: **gliss. weisse —**, glissando on the white keys,
    gliss schwarze —, glissando on the black keys: Schollum 7
    Fantasies 6; Scho. Op.11(1) **die — tonlos niederdrücken**,
    depress the keys soundlessly
tema/i (It.) theme (with set of variations): Liszt *Robert le Diable*
    due — marcato, stress both themes; Liszt *Sonnambula* **ben**
    marcato i due —, stress both themes
temperoso (It.) stormy: Liszt *12 Grandes Études* (1)
tempest(u)oso (It.) stormy: Liszt trs. Chopin 'Die Heimkehr'
    prestissimo —
tempo (It.) time, rhythm: a tempo, in the time of the piece, in the
    original time: **a — 1**, back to the original time: Liszt
    Apparitions 3 **ausser —, senza —**, not in strict time; Albéniz
    Op.47 (6) **subito —**, suddenly back to time: Dussek
    Op.19(4) **— di ballo**, at a dance speed
tendre (Fr.) tender: Deb. *Prél*.6 **expressif et —**; Messiaen VR4 **—**
    et naif, tender and simple
tendresse (Fr.) tenderness
tenebroso (It.) dark, shadowy, gloomy: Scriabin *Études* Op.8(7)
    presto —, agitato; Prok. Son.2(3) **il basso —**; Medtner
    Op.11(3); Sho. Son.1 Op.12
teneramente (It.) tenderly: Liszt, trs. Mozart *Don Giovanni*
    dolce—, Gran. *Goy*.(1) **— e calmato**
tenerezza (It.) tenderness: Field Noct.8; Schum. Hum.Op.20,
    Op.111(3); Liszt *3 Concert Studies* (1) **con —**, tenderly, trs.
    Schub. 'Liebestotschaft' **appassionato —**

tenero (It.) tenderly: Franck Op.5 **dolce** —, sweetly and tenderly

tenuto (It.) hold: Beeth. Son.Op.19 **la sopra melodia molto** —, the upper tune well held; Son.Op.106(4) **ben marcato e** —; Liszt trs. *Tannhäuser* **il canto sempre un poco** —, always lingering a little on the tune

terzen (Ger.) third (interval)

tiefsinningen (Ger.) thoughtful, introspective: Liszt *HR5*

timbré (Fr.) toned, voiced: Poulenc *Mout.Perps.* **doucement** —; Deb. Prél.(2, 11) **doucement timbrées,** sounded gently

timbrez (Fr.) sound: Deb. Prél.2 — **légèrement la petite note,** sound the little note lightly

tirarsi (It.) drawing back, dragging: Beeth. Var.Op.120

toccata (It.) piece with rapid finger-touch: Schum. *Toccata* Op.7; Deb. *PP* 3

Tod (Ger.) death

tombeau (Fr.) tomb

tomber jusqu'à l'affaiblissement (Fr.) fall down until faint: Satie *Le Fils des Étoiles*

Tonadilla (Sp.) light song: Gran. *Goy.*(1)

Tonart (Ger.) mode

tonlos (Ger.) soundless, noiseless(ly)

Tonskalen (Ger.) scales

Tonwiederholung (Ger.) repetition, repeated notes

Torheit (Ger.) folly, stupidity

tornando (It.) turning: Bartók *Mikro.*144; Barber Noct.Op.33 — **al tempo,** returning to previous time

tosto (It.) rather: Liszt *HR1* **la mano destra piu** — **legato,** the right hand rather more smoothly; *A de P* 2 **piu** — **ritenuto** rather more held back

Toten (Ger.) the dead: Mouss. *Pict.*(8) **mit den** — **in toter Sprache,** with the dead in the language of the dead

toujours (Fr.) always

tourbillonnant (Fr.) whirling as in a whirlwind: Scriabin Son.Op.62 **ailé** —, in flight, whirling

tout à fait (Fr.) completely: Poulenc *Improvisation* — **sans Pédale,** completely without pedals

tout entier (Fr.) all together: Satie *Pièces Froides*

tr. (It.) trillo, trill: Scho. Op.23(5) **quasi** —, like a trill, but slower

tragico (It.) tragically: Scriabin Prél.Op.31(3)

tragique (Fr.) tragically: Scriabin Son.Op.66

traîné (Fr.) lagging behind: Deb. Prél.116

traîneau (Fr.) sleighing, sledging: Satie, title, 'le —'

traîneaux (Fr.) sledges, sleighs: Tch. Op.37a

traîner (Fr.) drag: Poulenc Noct.1; *Improvisation* 10 sans —

Trällerliedchen (Ger.) humming song: Schum. *Alb.Y.*(3)

tranquillamente (It.) peacefully, calmly: Chopin, Liszt, Fauré, Grieg, Busoni

tranquille (Fr.) peaceful: Deb. Prél.14; Liszt Fanta. Op.2 piano —

tranquillo (It.) peacefully, calmly: Bach/Busoni *Chaconne*; Bartók, Beeth., Brahms, Chopin, Clementi, Dvořák, Gran., Grieg., Liszt, Medtner, Mn., Mouss., Poulenc, Prok., Rach., Schub., Scriabin, Schum., Tch.; Busoni *Fanta Contrappuntistica* — misticamente

trattenuto (It.) held back: Barber Noct.Op.33

Trauer (Ger.) mourning, grief, sorrow

Trauergesang (Ger.) song of mourning, dirge: Grieg Op.17(14)

Traum (Ger.) dream: Schum. *Fant* Op.12, title, 'Traumes Wirren', restless dreams

Träumerei (Ger.) dreaming, reverie; Schum. *Ksz.*; Tch. Op.39(20); R. Strauss Op.9

Traumeswirren (Ger.) restless dreams, confused thoughts of a dream: Schum. *Fant* Op.12, title

Traumgesicht (Ger.) dream vision

tre corde (It.) three strings, i.e. cease to apply soft pedal

tremendo (It.) trembling: Liszt *Apparitions* leggierissimo —, very lightly trembling. Tremolando is also used extensively by Liszt for similar effect

trémulo (Fr.) tremolo: Ravel *Miroirs* un — très fondu, a very fluid tremolo

trio (It.) short piece in 3/4 time, normally placed between two minuets (*see* menuetto)

Triolen (Ger.) triplets

triolets (Fr.) triplets

triste (Fr.) sad: Deb. Prél. 10, 11, 16, très calme et doucement —

tristemene (It.) sadly: Prok. Son.2(1)

tristesse (Fr.) sadness: Satie *Gnossienne* (6) avec une — rigoureux, with a strict sadness

tristeux (Fr.) sadness: Prok. Son.2(3)

tristezza (It.) sadness: Deb. *Études* 3; Smetana Op.2(2); Grieg

Op.66(7); Prok. Son.2(3) **con** —, sadly

troika (It.) Russian coach and three horses abreast: Tch. Op.37a

trombe/a (It.) trumpet: e.g. Scriabin Son.Op.53 **quasi** — **imperioso**, like an urgent trumpet; Busoni *Fanta contrappuntistica* **quasi** — **dolce**, like a soft trumpet

trop (Fr.) too much

troppo (It.) too much, as in **allegro non** —, not too fast

Turmuhr (Ger.) tower turret clock: Schum. *Pap*.Op.2

tutte le corde (It.) *see* **sordini**. All the strings (as opposed to the **una corda** of the soft pedal): Mn Son.Op.6 **poco a poco** —

——U——

umherschweifen (Ger.) wander about, roam

Umkehrung (Ger.) inversion

una corda (It.) one string (soft pedal): in the modern grand piano, one, two or three strings for each note are struck according to the pedals depressed, and this produces distinct tones as well as degrees of volume. In the upright piano, the operation of the soft pedal does not affect the number of strings struck, but the distance moved by each hammer to strike a string. The difference is then more simply one of volume than strictly of tone. The partial sounding is contrasted with the removal of the dampers for all strings if the sustaining pedal is used. In earlier pianos, and the mid-bass of modern pianos, the notes tended to be bi-strung, so that the **una corda** pedal did indeed reduce functioning to one string. *See also* **soft pedal**

ungeduldig (Ger.) impatient: Schum. *Davidsbündler* (4)

ungefähr (Ger.) rough, approximate

uniform (Fr.) uniform, even: Poulenc *Suite* (2), Imp.5

un peu cuit (Fr.) cooked lightly, medium rare: Satie *Danses de Travers* (2)

unruhig (Ger.) not quiet, disturbed, restless: Brahms Op.76(1)

unruhigbewegt, restlessly disturbed/moved
Unschuld (Ger.) innocence: Smetana, title
Unterirdischen (Ger.) subterranean goblins
unvollendete (Ger.) unfinished: Schub. Son.C maj. (1825),
'Reliquie'

vagamente (It.) vaguely, cloudily: Scriabin Prél.Op.33(2)
vague (Fr.) misty: Scriabin Prél.Op.67(1); Albéniz *Iberia* très, très
—
Vallée des Cloches (Fr.) Ravel *Miroirs*(5), title
valeur (Fr.) value, worth: Deb. Prél.2(1) **la main gauche un peu
en — sur la main droite**, the left hand a little stronger than
the right; *Images* (1) **le thème en — et soutenu**, the tune
emphasised and sustained
valzer (It.) waltz: Prok. Son.Op.82(3) **tempo di — lentissimo**, in
a very slow waltz time
Varsovian (Fr.) of Warsaw: Chopin *Waltz* Op.69
vecchio (It.) old: Mouss. *Picts.*
veille (Fr.) is awake: Messiaen VR19
veloce (It.) with velocity, headlong: Schum. Son.Op.11(4) **brillante e —**; Liszt* HR1 **legatissimo**; *Apparitions* (2) **— delicato**; trs. *Don Giovanni* **— glissando**; Poulenc
Improvisation (8)
velocissimo (It.) with extreme velocity, headlong: Liszt *12
Grandes Études* (5) **leggerissimo, —**, very light, extremely
fast
velocità (It.) speed, velocity: Gottschalk *Bamboula* **con —**
velouté (Fr.) velvety: Scriabin *Piéces* Op.56(3)
verbreiten (Ger.) broaden: Hindemith Son.3(4)
verhallend (Ger.) fading away: Schum. Op.133(5)
verklärt (Ger.) bright, radiant: Liszt *Gretchen*
verklingen (Ger.) die, fade away: Schollum 7 *Fantasies* (3) **—
lassen**, let it fade away
Verlauf (Ger.) course, progress

Verlust (Ger.) loss: Schum: *Alb.Y.*(16)

veröffentlicht (Ger.) published

vers (Fr.) towards

Verschiebung (Ger.) the pushing of the hammers sideways (by the soft pedal) so that they do not strike all two or three strings (in a grand piano)

verstummt (Ger.) becomes silent, ceases: Schum. *Pap.*Op.2

vertige(It.) vertigo, dizziness: Scriabin Son.Op.53(1)

vertiginoso (It.) dizzy, giddy: Scriabin Son.Op.53(1)

Versuckung (Ger.) holding back, delay: Liszt *12 Grandes Études* (6)

vibrant(e) (It., Fr.) vibrating, throbbing: Liszt *Apparitions* (3) — **delirando**, deliriously vibrating; *12 Grandes Études* **energico** —; Franck, *Eclogue* Op.2

vibrer (Fr.) vibrate: Deb. Prél.2., *Études* 12, *Epitaph* 5 **laisser** —, allow to vibrate: Messiaen *VR*16; Deb. *Images* (2) **faites** —

viel (Ger.) much

vierge (Fr.) virgin

Viertel (Ger.) quarter: Liszt. trs. *Flying Dutchman* **pedal mit jedem** —, pedal with each of the four beats

vigoroso (It.) vigorous: Liszt Fanta.Op.2

vingt (Fr.) twenty: Messiaen, title, — **Regards sur L'Enfant Jésus'**, Twenty Studies of the Young Jesus

visionario (It.) visionary: Busoni *Fanta. on Carmen* **andante** —

vitesse (Fr.) speed: Poulenc *Improvisations* 6 **à toute** —

vivace (It.) lively, spirited (hence fast): **molto** —, extremely fast; Mn Op.7(5) **poco à poco** —; Britten *Holiday Diary* (1) — **ma non troppo presto**, lively but not too fast

vivacissimo (It.) very lively: Beeth. Son.Op.81a, Schum. Son.Op.14(3); Bartók *Mikro*. 142, 146; Liszt *HR*10 — **giocoso**

vivacità (It.) vivacity, life: Brahms, Handel Var.Op.24(7); Clementi Son.Op.24(3) **con** —

vivamente (It.) lively, with spirit: a favourite of Liszt*, e.g. *Mephisto Waltz* 3, *12 Grandes Études* (9), *Grand Galop*

viviente (It.) becoming lively: Beeth. Son.Op.110(3), Deb. *Études* 6; Liszt Son.(1)B min.

vivo (It.) lively: Beeth., Chopin, Deb., Mouss., Martinů, Scriabin, Schum.

voce (It.) voice, internal part: Schum. Hum.Op.20 **innere** stimme, — interna; Scriabin *Poème* Op.32(1) **ben marcato le due** —, **ma dolce**, stress both parts, but sweetly

voglia (It.) desire, craving, longing, yearning: Scriabin Son.Op.30(1) **con** —, longingly

voilé(e) (Fr.) veiled, muffled: Scriabin Son.Op.70 **avec une ardeur profonde et** —, with a deep hidden passion

volando (It.) flying: Scriabin Op.30(2) **prestissimo** —; Op.53(1) **leggerissimo** —, very lightly flying

Volkslied (Ger.) folk-song

Volkston (Ger.) popular style, folk-song: Schum. *Alb.Y.*(41); Grieg Op.63(1)

Volksweise (Ger.) folk-song, popular tune

volta (It.) time: **una** —, once

volubile (It.) flowing: Deb. *Études* 3

volupté (Fr.) pleasure: Scriabin *Poème* Op.61 **avec une — dormante**, with a sleeping pleasure; Son.Op.70 **avec une — douloureuse**, with a gloomy pleasure

voluptueux (Fr.) voluptuous, sensual: Scriabin *Morceau* Op.52(2) —, **charmé**

vorher (Ger.) previously: **wie** —, as before

Vorspiel (Ger.) prelude

vortrag(en) (Ger.) delivers, presents: Schum. *Albumb.*(9) **leich-lich vorzutragen**, to be played lightly

W

Wächterlied (Ger.) watchman's/guard's song

Waisenkind (Ger.) orphan: Schum. *Alb.Y.*(6)

Waldespfad (Ger.) forest path

Waldesrauschen (Ger.) rustling woods

Walze (Ger.) barrel or cylinder for a barrel organ

Walzer (Ger.) waltz: German dance in triple time with the first beat stressed at the bass of the chord. There are fast and slow waltzes, and waltzes for piano were not necessarily intended for dance performance

wärme (Ger.) warmth: R. Strauss Op.9

warum? (Ger.) Why?: Schum. *Fant.*Op.12, title
wechseln (Ger.) change, alternate
weich (Ger.) soft, gentle, tender: Liszt trs. 'Isoldes Liebestod'
Weinleszeit (Ger.) vintage time, harvest: Schum. *Alb.Y.*(33), title
Wellenbewegung (Ger.) motion of the waves
wenig (Ger.) little, not much
werden (Ger.) become: Scho. Op.23 **allmählich langsamer** —, become gradually slower
wichtige Begebenheit (Ger.) important event: Schum. *Ksz.*(6)
wie (Ger.) as, like: — **ausser Tempo**, as if out of time, **rubato**
wieder (Ger.) again
Wiederholung (Ger.) repetition: **oftmälige** —, frequent repetition
Wiegenlied(chen) (Ger.) (little) cradle song, lullaby: Schum. *Albumb.*(6)
Wien(er) (Ger.) Vienna, Viennese
Wirre (Ger.) disorder, disturbance: Schum. *Fant.*Op.12 'Traumeswirren'
Wochenmarkt (Ger.) weekly market: Mouss. *Pict.*(7), title

——Z——

zart (Ger.) tender: Berg, Brahms, Schub., Schum., Scho., R. Strauss
Zeichen (Ger.) sign, mark (particularly the section mark 𝄋)
Zeit (Ger.) time
Zeitmass (Ger.) speed, measure
ziemlich (Ger.) rather
Zigeuner stil (Ger.) gypsy style: Liszt *HR7*
Zigeunertanz (Ger.) gypsy-dance: Schum. Op.118(3)
Zingarese (It.) gypsy: Liszt *HR11* **allegro** —
Zug (Ger.) procession, train
zurückhaltend (Ger.) holding back: Schum. Op.23, Op.118(1, 3), Op.133
zweimal (Ger.) twice: Liszt trs. *Flying Dutchman* **pedal** — **jeden Takt**, twice in each bar
Zwerge (Ger.) dwarf, pigmy

Composers

Albéniz, Isaac Manuel Francisco	1860–1909
Bach, Carl Philip Emmanuel	1714–1788
Bach, Johann Sebastian	1685–1750
Barber, Samuel	1910–1981
Bartók, Béla	1881–1945
Beethoven, Ludwig van	1770–1827
Berg, Alban	1885–1935
Brahms, Johannes	1833–1897
Britten, (Edward) Benjamin	1913–1976
Busoni, Ferruccio Benvenuto	1866–1924
Chabrier, (Alexis) Emmanuel	1841–1894
Chopin, Fréderic François	1910–1949
Clementi, Muzio	1752–1832
Debussy, Claude Achille	1862–1918
de Falla, Manuel	1876–1946
Dvořák, Antonin	1841–1904
Elgar, Sir Edward William	1857–1934
Fauré, Gabriel Urbain	1845–1924
Field, John	1782–1837
Franck, César Auguste	1822–1890
Granados (y Campina), Enrique	1867–1916
Grieg, Edvard Hagerup	1843–1907
Haydn, Franz Josef	1732–1809
Hindemith, Paul	1895–1963

Ireland, John Nicholson	1879–1962
Janáćek, Leoš 1854–1928	
Kuhlau, Friedrich	1786–1832
Liszt, Franz Ferenc	1811–1896
Lutoslawski, Witold	1913–1994
MacDowall, Edward Alexander	1860–1908
Martinů, Bohuslav Jan	1890–1955
Medtner, Nicholas	1880–1951
Mendelssohn (-Bartholdy), Felix Jakob	1809–1847
Messiaen, Olivier Eugène	1908–1992
Moussorgsky, Modeste	1839–1881
Mozart, Wolfgang Amadeus	1756–1791
Poulenc, Francis Jean	1899–1963
Prokofiev, Sergei	1891–1953
Rachmaninov, Serge	1873–1943
Ravel, (Joseph) Maurice	1875–1937
Saint-Saëns, (Charles) Camille	1835–1921
Satie, Erik Alfred	1866–1925
Schönberg, Arnold Franz	1874–1951
Schollum, Robert	1913–1987
Schubert, Franz Peter	1797–1828
Schumann, Robert Alexander	1810–1856
Scriabin, Alexander Nicholayevich	1872–1915
Shostakovich, Dimitri	1906–1975
Sibelius, Jean Julius	1865–1967
Sinding, Christian August	1856–1941
Smetana, Bedřich Friedrich	1824–1884
Strauss, Richard George	1864–1949
Stravinsky, Igor Fyodorovich	1882–1971
Tchaikovsky, Pyotr Ilych	1840–1893
Weber, Carl Maria von	1786–1826
Webern, Anton von	1883–1945

Abbreviations

Abegg. Var.	Schumann *Variations über den Namen Abegg*
A de P	Liszt *Années de Pèlerinage*
Albumb.	Schumann *Albumblätter*
Bach-Busoni *Chaconne*	J.S. Bach *Chaconne in D minor* arr. by Busoni
Bag.	Bagatelle
Ball.	Ballade(n)
Beeth.	Beethoven
Brahms Pag. Var.	*Variations on a Theme by Paganini* Op.35
Brill.	Brilliant
BB	Schumann *Bunte Blätter*
Busoni, *Carmen*	*Kammerfantasie über 'Carmen'*
Cahier	Debussy *Un Cahier D'esquisses*
Cap.	Capriccio
Ch. Corner	Debussy *Children's Corner Suite*
Conc.	Concerto
Davidsbündler	Schumann *Davidsbündler* Op.6
Deb.	Debussy
EET	Liszt *Études d'Éxecution Transcendent*
EETF	Liszt *Études d'Éxecution Transcendent d'après Paganini*
Eng.	English

Esc.Rom.	Granados *Escenas Romanticas*
Esc.Poet.	Granados *Escenas Poeticas*
Ét.Symp.	Schumann *Études Symphoniques*
Ét.Tab.	Rachmaninov *Études Tableaux*
Fasch.	Schumann *Faschingschwank aus Wien*
Fant.	Schumann *Fantasiestücke*
Fanta.	Fantasia
Fanta. on Carmen	Busoni, *Kammer-Fantasie über 'Carmen'*
FdJ	Messiaen *Fauvette des Jardins*
Fr.	French
Franck, *Prel.*	*Prelude, Chorale and Fugue*
Franck, *Ballade*	*Ballade* Op.9
Gaspard	Ravel *Gaspard de la Nuit*
Ger.	German
Gran.	Granados
Gran. Goy.	Granados *Goyescas*
Händel Var.	Brahms *Variationen und Fuge über ein Thema von Händel*
Hob.	Hoboken
HPR	Liszt *Harmonies Poétiques et Religieux*
HR	Liszt *Hungarian Rhapsody*
Hum.	Humoreske
Hung.	Hungarian
Imp.	Impromptu
Int.	Intermezzo
It.	Italian
K.	Köchel
Kreis.	Schumann *Kreisleriana*
Ksz.	Schumann *Kinderszenen* (Op.15)
L.	Latin
Liszt *Fanta.* Op.2	*Hungarian Fantasia*
Liszt *Grettchen*	2nd 'Character Picture' from *A Faust Symphony* 1874

Liszt *Soir*	*Soirées de Vienne*
Lut.	Lutoslawski
Lut. *Alb.Y.*	Lutoslawski *Album for the Young*, Folk Melodies (1945) ('The Lime Tree in the Field')
maj.	major
Maz.	Mazurka
Mikro.	Bartók *Mikrokosmos*
min.	minor
Mn	Mendelssohn
Mouss.	Moussorgsky
Mout. Perps.	Poulenc *Mouvements Perpetuels*
No.	Number
Noct.	Nocturne(s)
Nov.	Schumann *Novelletten*
Nw.	Norwegian
Op.	Opus
Overt.	Overture
Pag.	Paganini
Pap.	Schumann *Papillons*
PF	Shostakovich *Preludes and Fugues*
Pict.	Moussorgsky Pictures from an Exhibition
Pol.	Polonaise
Poulenc, *Suite*	*Suite for Piano* (1920)
PP	Debussy Pour le Piano
Prel./Prél.	Prelude/Prélude
Prok.	Prokofiev
Rach.	Rachmaninov
Ravel *Gaspard*	*Gaspard de la Nuit*
Ravel *Pavane*	*Pavane pour une infante défunte*
Saint-Saêns *Carnival*	*Le Carnival des Animaux*
Satie *Poésie*	*Poésie (Six Pièces de la periods* 1906–13 (3))
Scho.	Schönberg

abbreviations

Schub.	Schubert
Schum.	Schumann
Schum. *Alb.Y.*(28)	*Album for the Young* (28)
Schum. *Var.*	Brahms *Variations Über ein Thema von Robert Schumann*
Sho.	Shostakovich
Soir	Liszt *Soirées de Vienne*
Son.	Sonata
Son'a	Sonatina
Sp.	Spanish
Strav.	Stravinsky
Su.Berg.	Debussy *Suite Bergamasque*
SWW	*Songs without Words*
trs.	transcription
TrS.	Liszt *Transcendental Studies*
Tch.	Tchaikovsky
Tocc.	Toccata
Var.	Variations
VR	Messiaen *Vingt Régards sur l'Enfant Jésus*